THE
CATHOLIC
AS
CITIZEN

JOHN F. CRONIN, S.S.

HELICON

BALTIMORE · DUBLIN

Helicon Press, Inc.
1120 N. Calvert Street
Baltimore 2, Maryland

Helicon Limited
53 Capel Street
Dublin, Ireland

Library of Congress Catalog Card Number 63-12094

BX
1793
.C 7

(2)

Nihil Obstat: John F. Dede, S.S. Censor Librorum

Imprimatur: ✠ Lawrence J. Shehan, D.D.
Archbishop of Baltimore
May 8, 1963

The *Nihil Obstat* and *Imprimatur* are official declarations that a book or pamphlet is free of doctrinal or moral error. No implication is contained therein that those who have granted the *Nihil Obstat* and *Imprimatur* agree with the opinions expressed.

PRINTED IN THE UNITED STATES OF AMERICA BY
GARAMOND PRESS, BALTIMORE, MARYLAND

Contents

Introduction

Much is being said these days about the need for "engagement with the world." A Catholic should be apostolic, and his preferred area of apostolate is his immediate environment. He is a citizen of this world as well as a candidate for heaven. Our faith is a leaven as well as the precious pearl that must be safeguarded from harm. The call to charity in its fullest sense is absolute and imperious.

This book offers thoughts and suggestions on this apostolate. It is not a scientific treatise or a sociological study. It makes no pretense at being exhaustive or even comprehensive. Rather it reflects ideas that occurred to the writer as having value in modern America.

Had these chapters been written in the nineteenth century, undoubtedly they would have as a subtitle "Occasional Essays." Most of the material appeared as articles in *Our Sunday Visitor,* although revised and updated for book publication. Since they were written to be published as a book, however, they do have a certain unity of theme.

The suggestions given here center on aspects of the apostolate often overlooked or understressed. For example, our contribution to the ecumenical movement is seen in terms of the image portrayed by our lives as Christians. Others, more learned in Scripture, Liturgy, and Theology, have presented the vital function of these disciplines in the movement toward religious unity.

A recurring theme is the need for person-to-person involvement. All too often we lose sight of individuals in our commendable zeal for causes. Yet some of the most difficult problems in the modern world involve a loneliness and estrangement affecting many of our fellow men. The racial problem is not merely economic or political. It is a deep personal tragedy for many individuals and families. Juvenile delinquency is more than a social phenomenon; it is too often the reaction of those who are hurt and unloved. The Christian sees and seeks to heal the agonized souls of those afflicted by the ills of our society.

A reader familiar with the work of the Social Action Department of the National Catholic Welfare Conference may be surprised at the relative absence of economic topics. The economic subjects treated are mostly those tied in with current political problems. This selectivity was deliberate. It is much better to consider socio-economic problems in the context of Pope John's great encyclical letter, *Christianity and Social Progress (Mater et Magistra)*. A commentary on this historic document is in preparation.

REV. JOHN F. CRONIN, S.S.
Assistant Director
Social Action Dept., N.C.W.C.

ACKNOWLEDGMENTS

The author acknowledges with gratitude the kindness of the Rt. Rev. Monsignor Joseph R. Crowley, editor of *Our Sunday Visitor,* for his gracious permission to reprint articles which first appeared in *OSV*. He is also grateful to the editorial staff of Helicon Press, for unusual editorial assistance. Pressing administrative problems prevented the author from devoting as much time as he considers desirable to the work of revision and updating. The editors of Helicon Press filled this gap admirably.

I

As Others See Us

The Image of the Catholic

When Pope John projected the hope of Christian unity, he asked the help of all Catholics. We give this help first by prayer and penance, for the work of union will be above all the work of the Holy Spirit. But we can also help greatly by so living our faith that the image of the Church, seen in us, will be attractive and persuasive to the non-Catholic.

What is the true image of the Catholic? Leaving aside differences in national temperament and cultures, as well as in personal traits, there are certain qualities that should be outstanding in the true Christian. These qualities have been stressed in the Scriptures. They have been exemplified in the lives of the saints. Let us be specific and note the virtues and attitudes of the ideal Catholic.

The first and second laws of the Christian faith are love of God and love of neighbor. The distinguishing mark of the true Christian is love. Christ said this explicitly. This theme runs through the epistles of St. Paul and St. John. It has been characteristic of the saints. Putting the same idea in negative terms, a loveless religion, a religion of fear and dread, is but a caricature of the true Faith.

We love God because of his own goodness and because of his goodness to us. We address him as "Our Father."

9

The mark of the real father is strong love for his children. He is their support, their model, their guide. True, there are times when he must be stern in punishing the faults of his children. But even his function as judge is but a manifestation of love. He is protecting his children from faults and sins that harm the souls he values so dearly.

We love our neighbors—and to the Christian every man is his neighbor—because we see in them the likeness of God. Knowing that God loves them, we can do no less than try to imitate our heavenly Father. Every man is a child of God. He is called to be a temple of the Holy Spirit, a brother of Christ, a member of Christ's Mystical Body.

In effect this means that there is a sacredness about every human person. It often takes faith to accept this truth in the concrete and to apply it to the individuals we meet in our daily tasks. All too often we are made painfully aware of their failings. Many may seem to be weak, selfish, cruel, sensual. They seem to be sinners. We say "seem," because we can only observe their actions; God alone knows their souls. "Judge not, and you shall not be judged." "Forgive us our trespasses, as we forgive those who trespass against us."

Love of neighbor is strongly helped by a virtue that should characterize every Christian. We refer to the virtue of humility. Humility leads to selflessness, and love of self is a serious obstacle to love of God and love of neighbor. Humility at its best is not a morbid preoccupation with our own sins and failings. Awareness of sin helps us to be humble. But the real root of humility is a profound consciousness of our complete and total dependence upon God. What we have, we have received from him.

When we look at humility this way, we can see why the saints have always been the humblest of men. They are almost completely God-centered, and hardly at all self-centered. Hence they could sincerely use phrases that to us may seem exaggerated. They could speak of themselves as the lowest of men. They could be totally pre-occupied with the service of God, even to the point of apparent unconcern about their own salvation. Self means nothing to them; God is all.

A humble person turns spontaneously to prayer. Knowing his complete dependence upon God, he instinctively reaches upward for a guiding hand in every action. Of course, prayer for help and guidance is but part of our dialogue with our heavenly Father. Love, thanksgiving, and quiet contemplation are even more important aspects of prayer.

The Christian who walks with God is not a weak person. The uninformed think that humility and charity are not particularly manly virtues. That view can be corrected by reading the lives of saints and martyrs. The selfless person actually is far more courageous and decisive than the man who is always calculating what he might gain or lose in a given course of action.

Christian love and humility incline us toward tolerance and forgiveness. Our Savior forgave those who crucified him. St. Stephen prayed for his tormentors. If God and his saints can so act, we have a goal to follow. It is not an easy goal to achieve. The Sermon on the Mount was a call to heroism.

One of the most critical problems confronting the true Christian is his attitude toward evil, both moral and physical. We know that sin is a twofold evil: it is wrong primarily because it violates the law of God, our Creator, Redeemer, and loving Father. It is also wrong because it hurts us in our inmost being. It cheapens and degrades the soul that is the image of God. Actually, these two reasons are really one. God forbids pride, cruelty, selfishness, and the long category of human weaknesses because they are wrong in themselves. They are contrary to his goodness and holiness and at the same time destructive of the soul that he created.

We are told to condemn sin and yet love the sinner. Our Lord told the woman taken in adultery: "Neither will I condemn thee. Go . . . and sin no more." He did not condone the action—he called it sin—but he was kindly to the sinner. The parable of the Pharisee and the publican tells the same story. The prayer of the repentant sinner was heard. The selfrighteous boastings of the man proud of his virtue were condemned.

It takes all the delicacy of Christian love and humility to adopt Christ's attitude toward those whose actions are sinful. If we truly love the sinner, we can in no way condone conduct that hurts him and offends his Creator. Yet we must make it abundantly clear that our judgment is made "more in sorrow than in anger." We must not break the bruised reed nor quench the smouldering flax.

Robert Gleason, S.J., has some telling passages on this point in his perceptive book, *Christ and the Christian*. When he discusses the virtue of humility, he notes that some Christians seem to take great delight in looking for

12

evil and pouncing upon the weaknesses of others. Needless to say, such an attitude is not healthy. "Charity rejoiceth not in evil, but rejoices with the truth." Before every Mass the priest bows low in a confession of sin. If all of us made this confession from the depths of a humble heart, we would develop a correct attitude toward our fellow sinners.

There is another type of evil in the world which is called physical evil. It embraces the pain, sorrow, suffering, and death to which our fallen nature is heir. These evils, together with the suffering caused by the malice, thoughtlessness, or inadequacies of our fellow man, constitute the cross that Christ asked us to bear. Every Christian is "crucified with Christ." "If any man will follow me, let him take up his cross."

Here we note the paradox that, together with charity, makes the Christian unique. The paradox is joy in the cross. Our Faith is, of course, a religion of joy. This is one of the fruits of the Holy Spirit. No one can read the epistles of St. Paul, particularly the closing chapters, without noting his emphasis upon Christian joy in the Lord. Nor is this a message peculiar to the New Testament. The Psalms sing with the joy of faith and hope.

Where we differ from the unbeliever is that our joy not only survives sickness, suffering, and the other evils that constitute our cross, but actually thrives on them. How often have doctors and nurses been deeply moved by the patient, racked with the pain of cancer, whose lips move with prayer and who smiles with the joy of faith.

It is no accident that this happens. Suffering is a touchstone that profoundly influences the human character. It can make us bitter and self-centered. But it can also empty us of self and teach us mercy and sympathy. It can intensify love to the point of incandescence. The proud, independent, self-centered man can learn much from his bed of pain if he will pray.

It is harder to bear with mental suffering, such as that springing from unjust attacks, betrayal, neglect, indifference. But this, too, can purify us of self and bring us to even greater dependence upon the Lord as our everlasting Friend. And the saints can rejoice at the privilege of sharing the mental sufferings that surely are heavier and more cruel than the physical cross our Lord carried to Calvary.

Such, in brief, is the image of the devout Catholic. He is reverent, kind, tolerant, humble, joyful, and patient. If more of us aspired to this type of life, the Church would make a profound impact on the American scene. For a truly Christian life is more persuasive than learned books in testifying to the truth of our Faith.

The Image Distorted

In our first chapter we asserted that the movement toward Christian unity can be aided by the example of a true Christian life. Now it may be useful to examine distorted images of this life. These images can give a false, and often repulsive, picture of the Church.

Here we are not primarily concerned with the lax or indifferent Catholic. The discerning understand such a person. They know that it is unjust to blame the Church for those who, though professedly Catholic, are not really trying to live up to the ideals of the Faith. Nor will intelligent persons criticize the Church because of the weakness of members who suffer from deep-seated personality defects. Religion does not usurp the function of medicine. While faith may help the neurotic or psychotic, it is rarely sufficient of itself to cure him.

Our concern at this time is rather with the devout, perhaps even militant, Catholic who fails to comprehend the fullness of Christ's teaching. Such Catholics are usually zealous, faithful to the laws of God and the Church, and anxious to defend and even fight for the Faith. Yet their lives are distorted because they seize upon one or two truths and practices, to the exclusion of higher and more important truths and virtues. Again, let us be specific.

The first commandment is love of God. But do all devout Catholics savor the infinite love of our heavenly Father, the redemptive love of the Son, the message of the Spirit of love? Certainly this is not the case with those whose attitude toward God is almost exclusively one of fear. They consider their loving Father only as a terrifying judge. They are obsessed with worry over sin and dread of hell. If such persons happen to be in religion, they tend to develop this fear in those whom they teach.

There is, of course, a proper fear of the Lord. Sin and hell are dread realities. We need awareness of these realities, just as the child needs to be warned about dangers from fire, poison, and city traffic. But a home life that is purely negative, a home in which there is fear but not love, produces dwarfed and twisted personalities. Likewise, a spiritual life based only upon fear and avoidance of evil is stunted.

15

The highest degree of fear of the Lord is a mixture of awe and filial love. The devout and balanced soul avoids sin primarily because of reverent obedience to a loving Father. Even the thought of hurting One who is so good is unbearably painful. Such "fear" is like the concern of loving spouses who would suffer anything rather than hurt the one they love. They are faithful because of love, not because they dread the divorce court.

Our attitude toward the Sacrament of Penance (on either side of the screen) often shows the nature of our fear of the Lord. Penance is primarily a sacrament of mercy. It should be a source of solace, of consolation, of encouragement. Through it Christ gives us forgiveness and the strength and grace to avoid evil. The humiliation involved in confessing sin should spur us to greater reliance upon God and a turning away from self.

Another imperfection in regard to God is the concept that makes the Almighty a mere heavenly bookkeeper. Persons so inclined count their novenas, their pious practices and devotions, and their precisely calculated "acts" of virtue. Thus they pile up carefully measured "rewards" in heaven. Attitudes like this hardly reflect the selfless, uncalculating generosity of love. They can be occasions of pride. Sensible persons do not measure human love by the amount, value, and frequency of gifts offered. We should give because we love, not to purchase a reward.

Imperfect ways of loving God often lead to imperfection in love of neighbor. When we are morbidly and excessively preoccupied with sin, we often find it hard to be tolerant and forgiving toward the frailties of others. Since the most obvious signs of human weakness are sins of the flesh—anger, lust, and drunkenness—we are vigorous and vocal in denunciation of such sins. If the sinner is one of our own family, we may be merciless and unforgiving. If we are in religion, our sermons and instructions too often center around the single theme of avoidance of unchastity, as if this were the entirety of our religion.

How sharply this attitude contrasts with the practice of our divine Savior. He stated clearly the law of God on these matters, but the bulk of his teaching focused on love, prayer, and the more positive virtues. When he dealt with individual sinners, he was tolerant and forgiving toward those whose sin stemmed from weakness, and harsh and implacable toward those who were proud and cruel. Particularly revealing is what may be termed the "catechism of judgment." "I was hungry and you gave me to eat, thirsty and you gave me to drink, naked and you clothed me. . . ." Again, he said: "Blessed are the merciful, for they shall find mercy."

To avoid misunderstanding, let us reassert that serious sin is death to the soul. Drunkenness and impurity are as disastrous as pride and cruelty. Yet, humanly speaking, there may be reasons why sins of weakness may be repented, whereas sins of pride and cruelty may not be. The lecher and the drunkard are usually aware that they are doing wrong and are secretly ashamed. With kindness, they can be led to repentance and amendment. But the proud and cruel close their hearts to God and their fellow man. Since they do not acknowledge sin, it is far harder for them to repent.

Equally important is a proper attitude toward those who differ from us in faith and in specific religious prac-

17

tices. These differences may be partial, in the case of our fellow Christians, or almost total, in the case of doctrinaire Communists. How should the devout Catholic act toward such persons?

One attitude that is totally un-Christian is that of hatred. Hatred has no place in the Christian heart. We have been specifically told to love our enemies and to pray for our persecutors. Have we ever prayed for Hitler, or Stalin, or Khrushchev? In our quite legitimate concern about Communism, have we allowed the poison of hatred to fill our hearts? How would our actions fit in with the norm proposed by Archbishop John P. Cody when he was Bishop of Kansas City-St. Joseph: "Let us distinguish between the analysis of an opponent's ideas on the one hand and the labeling of an opponent's person on the other. Let us also learn the difference between criticism and condemnation, and let us observe how closely the Church restricts the power to condemn."

A very kindly, but far from timid, archbishop once told the author that in the ten years of his occupancy of an important see, he had never uttered a single word in public condemning those of another faith. He has maintained this rule in spite of some severe provocations. Even in the face of what was almost certainly bigotry and malice, he remained silent as Christ did before Herod, and he is by no means an exception.

If silence, or a calm and dignified defense of the truth, is the Christian ideal when confronted with the bigot and the persecutor, how much more so should we be kindly toward those who disagree without malice. It must be a shock and a scandal when a well-meaning Protestant or

Jew disagrees with a position of the Catholic Church, or even unknowingly misrepresents it, and receives in turn a torrent of personal abuse.

Unfortunately Catholics who act this way are usually quite vocal and "zealous." They miss no occasion to "defend the Faith." Nor are their victims only those outside the Church. They can be equally vitriolic and abusive toward their fellow Catholics who disagree with them. This is especially true when emotional social issues are involved, such as Communism, labor unions, and racial problems. Pope Pius XII explicitly warned against this abuse in his 1957 address to the Catholic Press Association of the United States:

> But in regard to questions on which the divinely appointed teachers have not pronounced judgment—and the field is vast and varied, saving that of faith and morals—free discussion will be altogether legitimate, and each one may hold and defend his own opinion. But let such an opinion be presented with due restraint; and no one will condemn another simply because he does not agree with his opinion, much less challenge his loyalty.

A cynic once remarked that some people are so busy "doing good" that they have no idea of the harm that they are causing. Likewise, there is a type of "militant" defender of the Church who does incalculable harm to the cause of Christ. What this group lacks in numbers, it makes up in stridency and volume of statements and letters. How is the average non-Catholic to know that the image they present is a distorted image of the Church? Can he be blamed for fearing another Inquisition, should Catholics achieve majority power in the United States?

19

Even if he does not go that far, will he be attracted to the Church by outpourings of venom and spleen?

The Catholic Church is not a negative force. Its doctrine is not confined to three "anti's." It cannot be defined merely by stating that it is the church that opposes Communism, birth control, and divorce. On the contrary, throughout its history, in Council after Council it has rejected the views of those who tended to distort or oversimplify its message. It taught the reality of sin, but denounced the heresies that held that man is totally corrupt. It encouraged strong efforts to strive for virtue, but condemned as heresy the view that man does not need God's help.

But distortion does not need to go to the extreme of heresy to do harm. The heretic leaves the Church, and the Church is no longer held responsible for his views. It is far harder to explain the apparently devout and zealous Catholic who presents a distorted image of the Church. If he is obsessed by fear, intolerant of human frailty, and bitter and spiteful against his opponents, he will close the door that Pope John is trying to open. That would be tragic in a world already torn by fear and doubt, desperately seeking truth, and pitifully in need of the healing love of Christ.

Forming Christ's Image in Us

After discussing true and false images of the Catholic, the question arises: How is the image of Christ formed in our souls? It would hardly be possible in a short chapter to give an adequate answer to this query. But it may be useful to offer some thoughts that may inspire us to look more closely into this all-important subject.

First we should understand clearly what holiness means. Holiness is the love of God *above* all created goods and *in* all created goods. This means that we love God more than self, family, friends, and possessions. It also means that our proper love for these great gifts of God must be in a framework of gratitude toward the Giver.

Many persons misunderstand the real nature of holiness. Some view it negatively, as a mere absence of sin. Sinlessness is not enough. A humble, repentant sinner, anxiously seeking to love God, may be much holier than a person whose life seems blameless, but who lacks love. The repentant sinner is seeking God. The iron-willed but unloving person may be seeking only self.

There are those who view holiness in terms of spectacular events in the lives of the saints. But holiness is not extraordinary penance, or heavenly visions, or the gift of miracles or prophecy. These may be fruits of the love of God, but they are not essential. They are not even important in judging sanctity.

Finally, some consider holiness as reserved to those in the religious state. Christ thought otherwise. In the Sermon on the Mount, addressed to the multitude, he said: "Be you therefore perfect, as my heavenly Father is perfect." Most priests can reinforce this statement from their own experience. How often have we been awed at the deep faith, love of God, simplicity, and compassion in souls that we are directing! How often do we envy them their spontaneous goodness!

How does one get to love God deeply and make this

love a greater and greater part of life? The first step is the desire, the will to act truly as children of our heavenly Father, adopted brethren of Christ, temples of the Holy Spirit. Then there is prayer, asking the Holy Spirit to form Christ in our hearts. We ask God to teach us his ways, so that we can see him in all people and in all things. Gradually we realize that self and self-seeking are obstacles to this love. From this follows knowledge of the need for penance and self-discipline.

It should be relatively easy to see God in nature, and to thank him for his goodness. The beauty of sun and stars, of trees and lakes and mountains, of oceans and even solitary deserts—all this has drawn man's heart to the Creator of all good gifts. We should thank God also for the great works of man's hands, for the wisdom and artistic taste that produced them is but a small reflection of eternal Wisdom. The goodness that we find in our fellow man is his goodness. Human love is great and ennobling, and God gave us this gift.

We must learn also to find the ways of God in every happening of our life. This comes easy when his protection and loving Providence are evident in favors received and dangers averted. Our faith is tested more strongly when we are confronted with pain, suffering, frustration, and the apparent malice of some of our fellow men. These trials we must expect, as part of the cross promised to every follower of Christ. Love is purified and strengthened by suffering. Suffer we must; the only real test is our willingness to accept this in union with the crucified Lord.

The person who loves God tries to see his will in every

happening of life. To such a person, life is unified, not divided into separate compartments for secular and sacred. His work, his family, his joys, his sufferings, yes, even the humiliation of weakness and sin—all have a deep relationship to God.

Those whose calling is to family life have special opportunities for holiness. They share with God the miracles of creation. They have deep responsibilities in relation to spouse and children. They have many joys to thank God for, and many, many crosses to bear in union with Christ. Unselfish love should reign in the home, and unselfish love is one of the first fruits of love of God.

Many will find it difficult to see the hand of God in the harsh world of work. Here is competition, conflict, struggle, selfishness, greed, coldness, pride, and cruelty. Perhaps this is the case. Perhaps our work will remind us of the Cross more than the Resurrection. But let us not be too quick in judging. "To the pure, all things are pure." "To those that love God, all things co-operate toward goodness." People react to other people. And as we show more and more, without our realizing it, our thoughts of God, others may slowly react the same way.

But we should seek God particularly among the unfortunate. The Gospels overflow with compassion. "I have pity upon the multitude." Christ came to save sinners. His miracles generally were those of healing. To the obdurate, he spoke of justice and judgment, but most of the time his discourses touched upon forgiveness and love. No human life is complete that does not include disinterested help to someone who is in trouble, whether this be sickness or poverty or sin. Needless to say, money given to charities is but a first step in this direction. We must give of ourselves, not merely of what we own.

Holiness of life is particularly helpful as our contribution to Pope John's plea for Christian unity. As we grow in love of God and neighbor, we spontaneously tend to see goodness in other people. Our separated brethren in the Christian Faith—Orthodox and Protestant alike—will be to us what Pope John called them in his first encyclical: our brothers in Christ. While holding fast to the Faith as God gave it to us, we will nonetheless respect the many excellent qualities in those who are not of the Faith. We will honor their uprightness, their prayer, their compassion, their deep reverence for the revealed Word of God in the Holy Bible.

The work of Christian unity must be a work of the Holy Spirit. Scholars can help by their learned discussions. It is useful to remove prejudice based upon misunderstanding. Common work in community enterprises of compassion and public morality tends to generate mutual respect. But unless a spirit of love and humility pervades all these and other contacts, it is unlikely that they will bring us more closely together. Indeed, if they are poisoned by pride and arrogance on our part, the breach could be widened.

The Catholic who is seeking to love God more will find great help in the practice of regular reading of the Holy Bible. Those not familiar with the inspired Word of God may find the thousands of pages formidable and forbidding. It would be well to begin with buying the New Testament and the Psalms, separately. Most persons prefer one of the better modern translations, since the language is more like that of everyday life. A good Catholic bookstore will have a choice in this matter. By comparing the same passage in several translations, say the fifth Chapter of St. Matthew's Gospel and the twenty-third Psalm, it is possible to choose the version that appeals most to the individual purchaser.

In reading the New Testament or the Psalms, there is no need to be worried about failure to understand certain passages. Many historical references or allusions to current events are not clear to the average modern reader. What is important is to read and read again, and underline, the words of our Lord, of St. Paul, of St. Peter, of St. John. Reading of this nature helps in prayer. And let us not forget that the Psalms are the heart of the Divine Office, the official prayer of the Church.

It is also helpful to have some spiritual books. They can be as relaxing as television, and infinitely more helpful. Those who may be interested in lives of the saints should seek advice on the more modern and better written lives. Some biographies of the saints give a distorted and sugary image of these heroic souls.

Finally, a word about prayer. Prayer is talking with God. It is more than asking favors. It is thanksgiving, reverence, love. We need not go to church to pray. Indeed, a good way to end our day is to spend a few minutes reading the New Testament and a Psalm or two, plus a few more minutes in quiet thought about God. We will find that the practice of prayer tends to spread, and that idle moments during the day give us occasions for thinking of our heavenly Father. Prayer as we wait for that traffic light to turn green, or for the visitor to be shown in, or as we walk to the store can bring us closer to God. Thus grows the love that is holiness. Thus the Holy Spirit forms Christ in us.

In considering these ideas, we assume of course that the devout soul is faithful to the sacraments, the liturgy, and the traditional devotions of the Church. These help us grow in God's love. And the soul that loves is more fervent at Mass and in reception of the sacraments.

II

The Catholic in Community

Forming Christ's Image in Society

One of the most difficult problems faced by the Christian is that of his relation to the world. The teaching of the New Testament on the world is complex. It is so intricate that to superficial readers certain passages seem to contradict others. Our Lord and St. Paul often warn against the world. The Apostles were told that they were not of this world, as the Lord himself was not of this world. The world is often treated as synonymous with the forces of evil that would destroy the Christian way.

On the other hand, the Apostles were sent to teach all nations, to convert the world. They were to search out the lost sheep, to welcome home the prodigal son. At the very beginning of the Apostolic era, some of the first Christians did not fully understand their mission. Apparently St. Peter needed a direct divine revelation to realize that the pagan world was to be welcomed into the Church, without first going through the preparatory stages of Jewish practice. St. Paul, of course, was pre-eminently the apostle to the pagan nations.

Throughout Church history, the problem of relationship with the world arises again and again. Many failed to understand the complexity of Christ's teaching on this matter. They said that the world and mankind were totally evil and corrupt. This view was condemned by the Church. Yet some refused to submit and were expelled as heretics.

Error arose also from the other extreme. There were those who underplayed human weakness and original sin and sought to achieve perfection without God's help. Some oversimplified the world's problems, seeking salvation only through works of political and social reform. Marxist socialism and communism are extreme instances of this error. Even good Christians sometimes become so obsessed with activity that they neglect their only ultimate source of strength, prayerful dependence upon God. "Unless the Lord build a house, they work in vain who build it."

The true Christian is in the world, but not of it. His love for his fellow man is without limits, but he does not accept the standards and principles of the world. The world, as defined in this context, has as its standards the seeking of self, of wealth, of power, of pleasure. These are considered as goals that are good without qualification. The Christian, on the other hand, can never accept such goals as absolutely good. Some of them have their qualified uses. All of them can be dangerous.

Yet we cannot avoid the temptations of the world by withdrawing from it. This would negate the virtue of love of neighbor as well as Christ's mandate to convert the world. Even those who live lives of secluded contemplation in cloistered orders do not withdraw from the world. As they grow in love of God, they grow in love of neighbor. They may manifest this love through prayer rather than through an active ministry. Even so, many of our greatest contemplative saints have been extraordinarily active. What woman, even in these days of feminism, affects contemporary society as did St. Teresa of Avila? Yet her first vocation was to reform the Carmelites and to restore primitive austerity and detachment to that order.

Apostolic contact with the world can and should take many forms. First, there is the direct teaching of religion by word and example. Missionaries, radio and TV speakers, and leaders of information centers are good examples of this approach. A second approach might be called teaching through compassion. Those who minister to the sick, the poor, the unfortunate of all types are practicing love of neighbor. If this is done for love of God, it can win souls. The purely professional doctor, nurse, and social worker can do much good. But when genuine love supplements technical skill, the result can be apostolic.

Finally—and this is the special aim of the present book —there is the effort to form the image of Christ in society itself. By society is meant the powerful permanent associations that men are wont to form, such as the family, the neighborhood, the community, the nation, world political society, economic units, and related groupings. These societies deeply affect the lives of each of us. This is obvious when we compare sharply contrasting societies, such as our own and those of a Communist nation.

The late Pope Pius XII did not hesitate to say that social conditions can profoundly influence the lives of individuals. In June, 1941, he asked in a solemn radio address how the Church could "remain silent or feign not to see or take cognizance of social conditions which, whether one wills it or not, make difficult or practically impossible a

Christian life?" He said that "upon the form given to society, whether conforming or not to divine law, depends and emerges the good or ill of souls."

This judgment, and other similar papal statements, can be very helpful in clearing up confusion in some Catholic circles. Because Marxists, whether communist or socialist, go too far in emphasizing the effect of social and economic conditions, some of their opponents tend to swing to the other extreme. They underplay or ignore the impact of destitution, unemployment, racial injustice, slums, or labor-management strife upon the lives of individuals and families. Many social evils involve violations of justice or charity. Most, if not all, have an adverse impact upon our brothers, the struggling children of God.

Love of neighbor can, and often should, lead to interest in social reform, and to the consistent and intelligent effort to mold society according to Christ's image. In this connection, it is important to note the distinction between ordinary "works of charity" and social reform. Those who minister to the immediate needs of the destitute, the delinquent, the alcoholic, and many other unfortunates are doing a good and important work. "I was hungry and you fed me . . . in prison, and you visited me."

But it is equally important to seek to cure the underlying causes of social ills. We are not being ungrateful to the nurse who comforts a feverish patient when we ask for a doctor to give basic medication to cure the cause of the fever. In the same manner, we can appreciate the heroic work of our ministers of compassion—social workers, St. Vincent de Paul members, members of the Legion of Mary, and many others—and still wish for other apostles who will probe more deeply for causes and cures. These types of apostolic work are not in conflict; they are complementary.

Christian social action is concerned with the moral climate of society. It seeks to examine society in the light of Christ's teaching and the basic principles of justice and love of neighbor. Do the laws and customs of a society promote good and inhibit evil? Is there the needed organized effort to bring about a better moral climate? Is individual good will made more effective by intelligent and realistic programs?

The idea of *organized* effort, reaching into permanent molding forces in society—laws, customs, organizations— is central to Christian social reform. We assume, of course, that there is much individual good will, based on love of God and neighbor. We count heavily upon the power and example of leadership. But these alone are not enough to do the task.

We might trespass upon a future discussion to make this point less abstract. How is a parent to impress upon a teen-aged son or daughter the wisdom of sensible dating customs? First of all, the standard of discipline and piety within the home itself will be most important. The example and leadership of parents can be powerful influences. But will they be sufficient if the general standards of the neighborhood are lax and even dangerous? Will their children have the moral courage to defy the "code" of their companions and insist upon higher standards? Most parents can testify that this poses a real problem.

This is but one example among hundreds that could be given. An organized effort to put moral principles into the framework of society is helpful in at least two ways. It gives support to those who want to be good, but who lack the courage to fight against strong community patterns. And it constrains the evil-minded, by putting the force of social pressure, and even of law, against their carrying out their desires.

It is no easy task to embed sound standards in our society. Let us be frank: Catholics have not done too well in societies where there is but a single dominant Catholic culture. The problem is much more difficult here where we have not only religious diversity, but strong trends toward secularism in society. Catholics in New Orleans and elsewhere, resisting Church teachings on racial justice, illustrate how social and economic pressures may outweigh religious loyalty.

We have here a challenge of deep proportions. Meeting it may call for heroic love and holiness. So be it. None of the highly publicized problems of our day can be dismissed as trivial. The threat of nuclear war, the vigor of Communist growth, unrest among millions throughout the world, and the uneasiness that pervades our youth—any of these taken alone would be formidable. We face them all, and more. Great problems call for great men and women to solve them. We may not feel within ourselves this greatness. So much the better, if we but turn to Him whose power, and goodness, and mercy are infinite.

The Sanctuary of the Home

In our mission of bringing Christ and his love to the world about us, the home has a privileged place. It is a sanctuary of love and virtue. As such, it is the training ground for the apostolic Christian. But the home is a sanctuary in another sense as well. It is sacred ground to be defended from the intrusion of the irreverent and the profane.

Little need to be said in this book about the home as a school of character and virtue. There is abundant literature on this subject, as is evident from the selections in the reading list. We know that Christian parents must excell in unselfish love. We know that words are useless, unless backed by the power of example. We know that the best way to show love toward children is through kindly guidance, a discipline that gives them both standards and security. When this discipline is received in an atmosphere of love, not fear, it produces both strength of character and balance of personality.

But the work of the most devout, loving, and intelligent parents can be hindered, perhaps even nullified, by influences from without. While the home is the first and most effective school of virtue, it is not the only influence upon the child. The parochial or public school also affects his standards. The Church teaches and guides: its work is not exclusively sacramental. These influences generally supplement and intensify the work of the good Christian home.

There are other sources of influence that may not be helpful. Children learn a great deal from their companions. Pressures from this source are most critical during the period of adolescence. In these years, the problems facing the teen-ager are difficult in themselves. All at once and at the same time, youth is feeling its stirrings of independence, its first real drive to question and test authority and to strike out on its own.

These companions may come from homes whose standards are different from our own, and possibly dangerously lower. Or they may come from homes in which the proper combination of love and discipline is lacking. They may be rebellious, unsure, selfish, resentful. The teen-ager, already beset by his own problems of approaching maturity, finds his standards questioned from without. His ideals on such questions as dating patterns, the use of alcohol, willingness to work, and consideration for others when driving an automobile may conflict with those of his companions.

Home-inspired ideals may be challenged in other ways. The influence of motion pictures and television may be in the direction of sensuality, rather than Christian modesty and self-discipline. They breathe of a world with infantile notions of romance and an addiction to luxury, which is obsessed with superficial success rather than lasting achievement. There are those who, for the sake of personal gain, would debauch our society through the sale of filthy comic books and pictures.

The first protection against such corrosive forces is the strength of character and the guidance of the good home. Yet we pray often, "Lead us not into temptation." Is it enough to have high family ideals, if we do not also try to influence the environment that works to negate such ideals? We do not want hothouse children, shielded from all contacts with the world. But on the other hand we should not go to the other extreme and expose the immature to temptations that may overwhelm them.

34

Thus it is that parents today realize that they cannot fulfill their mission only within the four walls of their home. They must be concerned also with neighborhood and community standards. They must work together with others who share their ideals and strive to achieve wholesome community patterns.

Nor should the task be confined to the more obvious direct influences upon the personal morality of children. Sensuality, drunkenness, laziness, and reckless driving were but examples of the problems faced by the Christian home. There are others hardly less important.

A good current example is the problem of racial discrimination. This is a national, not a regional problem. In the South, it may show itself particularly in laws imposing discrimination in the schools. In the North, it is more likely to appear as discrimination in housing, job opportunities, and social contacts. We noted earlier that Christian morality means much more than chastity or sobriety. It is positive even more than it is negative. And love of neighbor, to say nothing of justice in his regard, is characteristic of the true Christian. A community that segregates and degrades on the basis of race or skin pigmentation has vicious and un-Christian codes written into its laws and customs. These attitudes also affect our children, assuming that at home they have been taught the Christian view of their fellow man.

Religious intolerance is also a problem that our children must face. As Catholics, they may be at times on the receiving end of bigotry and prejudice. But we would be less than honest were we to assume that Catholics were always victims, and never the perpetrators of bigotry. We differ in religious faith from Protestant and Jew. We differ in some articles of faith from the Orthodox Christian, but the main difference involves allegiance to the Holy Father in Rome. But religious differences should not be an occasion of hate or bigotry. They should rather be a challenge to us to win others by our kindness and gentleness, the while praying that the Holy Spirit will bring about a unity of faith.

Physical surroundings may influence the home. Even if our homes are not affected adversely, we must not be indifferent to the plight of others who are harmed by unwholesome living conditions. As Christians, we are our brothers' keepers. As prudent parents, we are aware that blight and degradation in any part of a community threatens everyone. Slum housing is a threat to Christian living. Referring to good housing, Pope Pius XII asked (July 24, 1949), "Can there be conceived a social need of greater urgency?" Children need adequate recreational facilities. If their energies lack wholesome outlets, they will find unwholesome and vicious escapes.

Parents certainly should be concerned about the quality of schooling available for the children of a community. Some families may be fortunate in having the best type of religious and academic teaching for their own children. This does not mean that they should neglect the needs of others not so blessed. Because Catholics strive for a parochial school system, there is a temptation to consider the public schools as outside our sphere of influence. But we have duties as citizens, as well as duties as parents. Moreover, the standards achieved in the public schools will influence our children, even though they are educated in religious schools. Community customs affect all alike.

Finally, we have no right to wash our hands of those in the community who lack the minimum standards acceptable in our society. Vice and delinquency are not merely police problems. Nor can prevention be left exclusively to social workers. We may not pass by our wounded brother lying by the roadside.

Obviously no single family can take extensive, direct, personal interest in every one of the problems outlined above. No one would have that much time available. Some would lack the ability to be helpful in more specialized situations. Yet each family must honestly confront the fact that the home is but one of many influences upon our youth. And if these outside forces are harmful, the work of parents may become almost impossibly difficult.

What then are we to do? Detailed suggestions on these and other problems will be given in later chapters of this book. But certain general thoughts may be useful, before going into details.

First, we must have the realization that the family cannot go it alone. Parents must work with other parents in the effort to secure sound community standards.

Second, we can get our greatest inspiration and strength in this effort from our own religious ideals. Hence problems such as those outlined here should be seriously discussed in appropriate parish or diocesan organizations. At times, we may need to consider the possibility of a new organization, if one does not already exist in our community. A Catholic interracial council would be an example. Another would be the introduction of the Christian Family Movement into our area.

Finally, we must give serious thought to the proper type of activity that will implement our ideals and programs. We may draw our inspiration and courage from our own personal faith. But many action programs will be successful only if they are carried out on a community basis. We must be prepared to work with others in our neighborhood or community, provided we can agree upon a program that is reasonably adequate.

In this way, we shall be taking our first steps toward forming the image of Christ in society. We shall move toward "restoring all things in Christ." The task just outlined calls for dedicated work on the part of families, already overburdened with many tasks. But if this work is not done, our problems of the future will be immeasurably greater, as a godless society corrodes the Christian home.

Parents as Shepherds

In the last chapter we noted the corrosive influences that can affect, and perhaps even nullify, the work of a good Christian home. This is a challenge to parents to unite in community action, so that wholesome rather than degrading forces form the environment that surrounds the home. Social pressures should be healthy, not disease-ridden.

As Christ is the Good Shepherd, constantly watching over his flock, so parents likewise are shepherds, guarding the souls that God entrusted to their care. Vigilance, love, and intelligent foresight can ward off the most serious dangers.

One of the first steps should be united action regarding the three "D's"—dating, drinking, and driving. In each situation, our youth tends to follow a pattern. The average youngster does not want to be different from his group. Many parents find it a difficult, often an impossible, struggle to insist upon standards higher than those prevailing in a given social pattern. The basic answer is to change the pattern.

Dating involves several problems. These include the minimum age for mixed parties, the suitable age for single dating, proper supervision of dances and parties, conduct after dances and parties, and hour for arrival home. Loose conduct in any of these areas exposes young people to serious emotional and moral problems, often beyond their ability to handle wisely. One of the most dangerous, in its effect upon later marriage, is premature steady, single dating. Apart from other considerations, this tends to narrow the range of choice, and hence the chances of finding a suitable partner.

The resources available for setting proper standards vary according to different community situations. Obviously dances held under the auspices of a parochial school are more likely to have proper supervision than those held by an informal group of teen-agers. But the parents usually have several allies in their efforts to keep sane ideals among growing boys and girls. The Church obviously is one. So are the schools, whether religious or public. Often teen-agers themselves can organize and work out suitable codes. Finally, parents can meet in some informal way to agree upon procedure for youthful dating.

If the social life of youth does not generally follow religious or parochial school lines, any effort at parental action should be on a broad, community base. We may well discuss these problems in Catholic societies, but a program of action should be more broadly organized. It is also much more likely to succeed if the young people themselves are included in the deliberations.

In this connection, better results are forthcoming if we stress the positive and not merely the negative. Too often these problems are dealt with in a very narrow fashion, with emphasis only upon danger of sin. Such a narrow approach may not be effective. It can have the unhealthy result of emotional identification of sex with sin, with consequent problems of adjustment in marriage. It also fails to convey the nature of sin itself. Immoral conduct is wrong not merely because God forbids it. It is more correct to say that God forbids it because it is wrong, and unhealthy for the souls of those indulging in it.

Community codes of conduct should emphasize the fact that healthy dating patterns, based on reverence for the partner and not upon the seeking of selfish pleasure, are the best preparation for happy married life. Such positive language also has an advantage in a wider community acceptance. Even the unbeliever, who may reject the notion of sin, could agree upon standards for sane preparation for marriage.

The same comments apply to drinking and driving. Here an added caution must be noted. Home example is likely to be an important factor in the attitudes of young people toward alcohol and automobiles. This is particularly the case when parents' standards are lower than the ideals they preach. If parents who drink do not do so in moderation, or drive with courtesy and caution, they are in a poor position to preach to their children.

The three "D's" involve problems that can be handled within a community. There are other influences upon youth that are more difficult to meet, since these influences come from outside the community. We refer, of course, to unwholesome television programs and motion pictures, and pornographic pictures and comic books. Generally, these are produced outside the community and sent in as a commercial venture.

There is no reason why the same groups that handle other problems involving youth should not be competent to act in this field. The Catholic Church, for example, is perfectly within its rights in judging the moral standards of motion pictures and literature. But it is often a mistake to make programs of *action* strictly Catholic. We can certainly assume that church-going Orthodox, Protestants, and Jews are equally concerned about these problems. Even parents who are not religious usually sense that commercial filth is unwholesome and demoralizing.

When Catholics "go it alone" in fighting these influences, others in a community are likely to be resentful. They do not like to be told what their moral standards should be. While any church has a right to fight for public morality, it is often more prudent and fruitful to make these programs community projects, rather than aims of just one religious group.

As a pattern of action, it might be well to distinguish between pictures, books, and magazines that are unacceptable for the young and those that may not cause problems to emotionally mature adults. Films and literature that should not be seen by children or youth can be handled by community action. Pictures for adults are usually best left to the consciences of individuals, guided by their Church ratings. If we try to ban such films, books, or magazines, we are likely to weaken the basis for community action in the more vital area of influences upon youth.

Community programs have an added advantage that they rarely involve boycotts, public condemnation, or other features that are likely to publicize evil and make it a subject of curiosity. If all the leading forces of a community work with theater owners, requesting that week-end films in neighborhood theaters be wholesome, or at least not morally objectionable, it is unlikely that their requests will be turned down. The same applies to newsstands selling comic books to the young. Outright pornography, on sale locally, is a police matter. A united community will get police action. Filth coming through the mails should not be destroyed but turned over to the postmaster for federal procedures.

We should not overlook the value of emphasizing the positive. If a particular television program is consistently wholesome, a letter to the sponsors will help keep it going. Of course, we can also tell the sponsors when we object to a program they support. But always we must be aware that we cannot merely object to what is evil. We must try to replace it with what is good. Young people are likely to rebel against a steady diet of prohibitions.

It is necessary to emphasize certain safeguards for the morals of our youth. But safeguards alone will not make strong character, any more than disinfectants alone will promote rugged health. Hence parents might also give much thought to positive standards and ideals that will challenge our youth.

One example is the discipline of work. Poverty imposed this upon most of the parents of present-day teen-agers. In many homes today, there is little economic need for children to work. But there may be a spiritual need for the character-forming influence of good, hard work, even —and especially—if it is not done for pay. Luxury and ease are often more corrosive than poverty.

In a world that has more and more comforts, it would be tragic to deprive children of the concept of sacrifice. This could be conjoined with religious practice, as Catholics, Orthodox, and many Protestants do during Lent and Advent. Or it could be tied to compassionate love of neighbor. Collections for the poor and unfortunate, such as the Bishops' Lenten collection, would be one example.

We should also try to challenge youth with higher ideals, preferably those involving personal participation in works of mercy and compassion. Few communities lack problems involving the sick, the poor, and the aged. Here are great opportunities for unselfish giving of one's time and effort. Here are purposive outlets for the restless energies of youth, not merely devices to keep them out of trouble.

While such programs of discipline and ideals should primarily stem from the home, they again can be strengthened by community interest. If the youth group can be interested in such activities, it is more likely that individual youngsters will go along.

Whether we like it or not, we are influenced by our surroundings. It is our task as parents and citizens to keep such influence healthful and positive. There is no guarantee that these measures alone will solve the problems of troubled youth. But they can contribute greatly to securing a better atmosphere to supplement the basic religious and moral training of home and Church.

Where Our Brethren Live

In pursuing the thought of the home and its surroundings, we must consider what is a Christian attitude toward housing and slums. Now naturally this problem of subnormal living conditions has its strongest and most direct impact upon the victims themselves; but it should also be a twofold concern of those whose housing is adequate and whose surroundings are pleasant and wholesome. For one thing, it appeals to their Christian love of neighbor, for the poor and the wretched are our brothers. In addition, the unsavory conditions fomented by slum living—delinquency, vice, and disease—cannot be isolated within a community. Crime and vice affect everyone.

Pope Pius XII wrote eloquently on the effects of poverty. He said in his 1952 Christmas Message: "For some families there is a dying daily, a dying hourly; a dying multiplied, especially for parents, by the number of dear ones they behold suffering and wasting away. . . . There is the weakening and consequent physical deterioration of whole generations. Whole masses of the population are brought up as enemies of law and order. . . . Not rare is the case where it is wretched misery that leads to crime."

In an address given on May 3, 1957, the Holy Father

again talked of the "exploitation of slum areas." "Enough can never be said about the harm that these dwellings do the families condemned to live in them. Deprived of air and of light, living in filth and in unspeakable commingling, adults and, above all, children become the prey of contagious diseases which find a favorable soil in their weakened bodies. But the moral injuries are still more serious: immorality, juvenile delinquency, the loss of the taste for living and for working, and interior rebellion against a society that tolerates such abuses, ignores human beings, and allows them to stagnate in this way and transforms them gradually into wrecks."

The Pope concludes that "Society itself must bear the consequences of this lack of foresight. Because it did not wish to prevent the evil and to provide a remedy in time, it will spend enormous sums to keep up an appearance of curbing delinquency and to pay expenses for prolonged confinement in sanatoriums and clinics. How many millions are authorized for the cure of evils that it would be easier and less expensive to prevent!"

These strong words of the Holy Father should shock the Christian conscience. For the cruel fact is that far too often we are ignorant of, or even unconcerned about, the conditions he describes. Some among us may react by feeling that the Pope had in mind European conditions that are not paralleled here. It would be comforting if this were the case. But there is hardly a large city in the United States which is not plagued with slums. There are rural slums also, and deplorable housing conditions for migrant workers. Minority groups, such as Negroes and Puerto Ricans, are especially victimized in this way.

Another reaction is the conviction that slum dwellers are merely suffering for their own shiftlessness. The Pope charitably labels those who hold this belief as "persons of good faith who have only an inadequate knowledge of the matter." The harsh truth is that slum conditions often are self-perpetuating. It is extraordinarily difficult for a new generation to rise above such surroundings, especially when limited educational opportunities condemn them to the wages of unskilled labor.

There is a vicious circle of demoralization in slums. Starting with the home itself, it is difficult to preserve any taste for beauty or respect for human dignity under conditions of intolerable overcrowding. Children have no place to study or play. They are driven to the streets, and thus to doubtful companionship and thousands of antisocial situations. It is all too easy, under such conditions, to turn to crime, vice, or hopeless apathy.

Some persons live in destitution because of inherent weaknesses. They may be mentally retarded. They may be inveterate gamblers or drinkers. They may be just downright lazy. It would be inaccurate to blame social or economic conditions for ills that may reflect psychiatric or spiritual problems.

Nor should we fall into the error of thinking that better living conditions will be an automatic solution for problems of vice and delinquency. Actually, some of the most publicized scandals of our time are found in our so-called better neighborhoods. Bored youths, accustomed to every luxury and lacking real home discipline, are often involved in the most vicious types of delinquency. Luxury can be just as demoralizing as destitution.

Perhaps we should say that the slum problem is really three problems. First, there are those who live in poverty because of physical or mental handicaps. Society seeks to help such persons largely through care procured by social workers. Then, we have the indigent whose difficulties are primarily spiritual. They are to be helped by the Church. Finally there are many who are trapped by a vicious environment. This group would develop and thrive if given better opportunities for education, housing, recreation, and jobs.

In view of the complexity of the problem, what should be the attitude of the true Christian who wishes to help his brethren in distress? It is easy to give a number of technical answers to this question, each with real merit. We could cite the work of case workers and clinics. We could note achievement in urban redevelopment and slum clearance. We could list advances in public housing and limited-dividend private housing.

All these fall into the category of techniques. They are useful, but their value is limited unless they transcend the technical and move toward the spiritual. The real curse of the slums is the feeling of hopelessness and rejection engendered in their victims. And this feeling can be combated only by apostolic interest in others as persons. This interest may be motivated by religion, or merely by a deep humanitarian interest in one's fellow man. But effective aid must be permeated by kindness and love, if we are to rebuild the spirit in those whose morale has been crushed and even apparently extinguished.

These observations explain why some programs fail and others, seemingly identical, succeed. Public charity may be abused, whereas St. Vincent de Paul work may have notable successes. The one may be impersonal, the other obviously motivated by Christian love of neighbor. Some social workers may be aloof, cynical, and disillusioned. Others view their difficult work as a real Christlike mission.

Many of the strongest advocates of public housing are painfully rethinking their positions today. They have found that better housing alone did not bring about better families. After fighting for adequate recreation areas, they found that these places made it easier for gangs to congregate. All this does not mean that the struggle for better housing and recreational opportunities was wrong. It simply indicates that it was only part of the problem.

The observation that we make here will recur as other social problems will be discussed. Social reformers rather understandably react to immediate evils. They want to protect the rights of labor. They seek better wages and working conditions. Even Catholics in this field have tended to concentrate onesidedly upon the seeking of justice. Yet the popes have constantly warned that justice alone is not enough. It must be warmed by the sun of Christian charity—the love of our neighbor as a person redeemed by Almighty God.

In the context of the problem under discussion, the steps open to the apostolic Catholic now seem clear. First, of course, we must learn accurately the nature of the problem we face. We must know techniques, ranging from ambitious programs of urban renewal to the unpublicized work of St. Vincent de Paul workers. But then comes the vital ingredient that the Christian can uniquely offer. This is concern for the individuals affected and a desire to help them as persons, not merely as abstract social problems.

This Christian spirit will gradually affect our techniques. We will consult people on their problems, and not merely impose solutions worked out by experts. We will be deeply concerned with methods that enable people to help themselves. Thus there will be considerable emphasis upon developing leadership from within slum neighborhoods. Perhaps new forms of education may need to be developed or existing ones expanded. For example, a Puerto Rican will have far more chance to get a job if he learns to speak English well. A Negro family, displaced from a Southern farm, may need technical training in order to secure skilled or even semiskilled jobs. In this human context, we would not break up neighborhoods ruthlessly when relocating families under slum-clearance projects. We would preserve and improve the existing community spirit.

A final point: Who is to do all this? Where a considerable amount of time and effort is called for, one thinks of retired persons or housewives with grown children. If the need is rather for facilities, then owners of factories, garages, and the like, could develop training programs. Details can be worked out. But the vital thing is that unfortunate Americans should be made to feel wanted and accepted. They should know that we really mean it when we call them our brethren in Christ.

III

The Catholic and Individuals

The Loneliest Ones at Christmas

Every Christmas season, two Dominican nuns drive their station wagon (donated by a Protestant gentleman) to visit the women's prisons in the Boston area. There they console and inspire some of the loneliest of God's children.

Spending Christmas in a long-term prison is bad enough. But some of these women have an inner loneliness far worse than prison bars. They are souls that came from homes without love. The only emotions they knew as children were fear and hatred. Adolescence brought them new problems and additional turbulence. But at no time did they learn the gentler emotions of love and trust.

It is hard to believe that another human being can say, "Sister, you talk of love of God and neighbor. But I actually do not know what love is. I cannot love anyone. I cannot trust anyone. From my earliest years all I can remember is fear and the conviction that I was not wanted.

"Perhaps I am here because I am bad. Possibly I knew no other way. I could never make friends. I shrank from meeting people in groups because I felt that I did not fit in and that they looked down upon me. Sister, do you know what it means to be lonely through and through?

50

to be lonely all the time? to be at your loneliest when you are in the midst of people?"

How often these Dominican Sisters have heard stories like these. And how readily the prayer comes to their lips: "Neither do I condemn thee; go and sin no more." But how to help this trembling, frightened woman? What future will she have when she leaves prison and returns to a world she cannot comprehend?

Let us look at this same woman ten years later. Again she is spending Christmas away from the world. But this separation is her own free choice. Instead of prison garb, she is now clad in the white robes of the Dominican Sisters of Bethany. Now she has a family, a family united by love, prayer, and penance. She is serene, relaxed, happy. The terrible wounds of the past have healed, and hardly a scar remains. This Christmas is unique for her, since she has made her final vows as a Dominican Sister.

The bell rings, calling the community to Midnight Mass. Postulants, novices, and sisters assemble outside chapel and enter in procession. The beautiful office of Matins precedes the coming of the little King. "Christ is born to us. . . . Come, let us adore him." In place of the bewilderment and fear of ten years ago, her heart is full of gratitude. "Christ is born," and this year she will receive "grace upon grace."

She is grateful above all to the divine Infant whose birth she now celebrates, and to his mother. It was to them that she prayed during those somber years, encouraged by the visits of the Sisters. They told her to pray for trust and love. They said that God would give her the fatherly love she never knew as a child, and that our Lady

51

would be her mother. It was so hard to believe this at the time, but she did pray. And her prayer of faith was heard.

As gratitude wells in her heart, she looks about her and thinks what her sisters in religion have meant to her. When she first met them, she felt that they were the kindest persons she had ever known. In fact, their love and compassion almost tore her apart. She wanted to trust them. At times she wanted to throw her arms around one of them and just sob "Mother, mother, mother." But the iron grip of fear kept her tender emotions frozen.

Now they are her sisters. And the prioress is the only real human mother she has ever known. Her sisters. She knows little about their past, since only superiors know the background of their subjects. But she has her woman's intuition. She knows that many, perhaps most, of her sisters came from normal homes. They had known love and security from childhood. They came to Bethany with spotless reputations.

But there were others, she feels, who shared her problems. Some had been in prison. Others had been in serious trouble, even though they had not committed crimes in the eyes of the law. But who could be sure? Here in chapel they were all one family. All wore the spotless white of innocence, and who could tell whether this was baptismal innocence, or innocence regained through prayer and penance?

Somehow, in Bethany the past does not seem to matter. Its founder said, "When he loves us and gives us his grace, God does not ask what we have been. He is only concerned with what we are." She knows that in a few minutes she will join her will with the will of Christ in the unending Sacrifice of the altar. In the morning there will be the Third Mass of Christmas day. She will have her half-hour of adoration before the Blessed Sacrament.

After the chanting of Sext, the Sisters will have Christmas dinner. Usually there is reading at meals, but in the United States talk is permitted at some big feasts, and especially on their first Thanksgiving and Christmas. From the beginning, the Dominican Sisters have insisted that their new foundation be truly American. The glorious spirit of Bethany is preserved, but European customs are adapted when found less suitable here.

At dinner, Sister felt that only the joy of heaven could surpass the happiness of her little community. Here was real love, a love that was especially tender because it was sanctified and consecrated to God. She knew that everyone had prepared special gifts for Sister Athanasia, since she would be receiving nothing from the outside world. Yet she also knew that this Sister would share the happiness of others, as they opened their mail and gifts from family and friends.

There were community gifts, too. An archbishop had sent some books that they particularly needed. The neighboring pastor dropped by with some beautiful Christmas records. And how could they ever repay the thoughtfulness of the other communities of sisters who seemed always to know what was lacking? She could only think of the phrase she heard so often as a postulant: "God is good, and we are his spoiled children."

She did not even mind the fact that she would not be called to the parlor during the Christmas season to receive the visits of parents and friends. She would be content to

share the joy of her sisters as they greeted their loved
ones. In a human way, of course, she would also like to
have such visits. But her family in religion has meant so
much to her that nothing else seems to matter.

Is the story just told real or fiction? So far as the United
States is concerned, it is partly fictional. It is true that
the Sisters take their station wagon to the prisons at the
Christmas season. But it was only recently that four
Dominican Sisters of Bethany came to start their first
foundation in the United States. While their convent was
being readied, they were guests of the Franciscan Missionaries of Mary at St. Clement's in Boston. Now they
have their convent, and have been blessed by their first
American postulants and novices.

But in another sense, the entire story is fact, not fiction.
Ninety-six years ago a Dominican priest, Father Lataste,
founded this contemplative community for the primary
purpose of praying for women prisoners. Some of the
sisters would be detached periodically to visit long-term
prisons for women. But the spiritual reservoir behind
these visits would be the prayer and penance of the entire
community.

He insisted from the beginning that his community
would accept women who have been in trouble, provided
that they had a true spirit of penitence and a sound desire
for the religious life. They would have a choice between
the somewhat simpler duties of a Dominican Tertiary or,
with proper permission, the canonical novitiate for full
profession. The distinction between the two states is not
based on the past history of any sister, but simply on her
current preparation and desires. A young woman with

a spotless record may choose to be a Tertiary. Another with a sordid past may accept the call to full profession.

In Europe some of their convents have annexes called pre-Bethany, where, if necessary, the candidates make a preparation of suitable length before entering the canonical or Tertiary postulate. The aim of the Sisters of Bethany is always spiritual mercy. In the words of their founder, "If they welcome souls, it is to save them; if they offer them family life, it is to help their perseverance, to encourage them, and to support that unconquerable strength which limitless charity gives to souls; it is to raise them gently and ever more and more to God."

In Europe there are also halfway houses, called Friendship Houses, connected with Bethany but run by lay women, not by the Sisters themselves. These lay friends, who are members of the secular institute "The Mission of Our Lady of Bethany," help women in trouble to make the transition from prison life, or any career that involves public disgrace, to a more normal life, either in the world or in a pre-Bethany home. These houses are also visited by the Sisters. There are no immediate plans for such houses in the United States, since it is first necessary to "fill the spiritual reservoir" by recruiting postulants for the religious life.

Christmas above all symbolizes God's infinite love and compassion. Our Lord seems to have a special compassion for public sinners who were repentant. And the soul of Bethany is compassion and love.*

---

* Those in any way interested in this unique foundation can get further information by writing the Dominican Sisters of Bethany, 19 Dartmouth Street, West Newton, Massachusetts.

Love and the Fearful

The discussion of Christmas at Bethany raises some interesting questions which should be explored more at length. This sister described in that chapter was fictional, but only in the sense that no individual known to this writer was concerned. The records of Bethany contain hundreds of stories just as remarkable as the episodes related.

Three essential points stand out in the lives of the lonely and the unloved. First is the fact that when a child does not receive love, it can happen that gentler emotions become frozen and may stay frozen throughout life. The second fact is that some of these persons turn to prayer and become genuinely and deeply religious. Finally, it has been observed that an atmosphere of real kindness and detached love has helped to unfreeze emotions and to bring about a normal development of personality.

The points just outlined have implications that extend far beyond the specialized work of Bethany. Many persons who cannot trust or love do not turn to lives of crime or vice. They may be our next-door neighbors, living perfectly respectable lives, but suffering the torments of inner loneliness. They too need understanding and help.

The wonder of Bethany lies in the strong contrast involved in its work. It deals with women who seem to have passed the point of no return. Yet it offers them the hope of an absolute reversal in their lives. The transition from prison or public scandal to a life consecrated to God by the vows of religion is indeed a miracle of love.

If such remarkable conversion can happen, surely there must be thousands of opportunities to help those who are withdrawn and lonely because of an all pervasive fear that makes real social relationships impossible. We miss these opportunities because we may lack the understanding and patience needed to help.

It is not easy to help victims of homes without love. They are usually so desperately afraid of the outside world that they cannot help but raise barriers to normal association and friendship. We must sense this situation, and with infinite delicacy and kindness show our trust and Christian love. It will not be returned at first, much as the person may wish to do so. Limitless patience must be practiced in addition to completely unselfish devotion.

We must realize that we are dealing with souls that cannot react normally to human contacts. To them, love and trust are just words, like red or green would be to a blind man. They face the world as aliens, learning by experience the proper reactions, but never having inner security.

With this deep-rooted and fundamental insecurity, many things can happen. Some never get into trouble. They retreat within themselves and try to avoid society. Often they find others like themselves, and prefer their company. If they marry, they cannot give their children the love which they do not feel. This can mean another generation of emotionally frozen souls.

Should they marry a person with normal emotions, the strain on the marriage is enormous. To the normal partner, they appear selfish, grasping, ungrateful. They try to dominate because they cannot understand. Once in a while the normal partner, because of deep love and infinite patience, wins their trust. Trust leads to the beginnings of love and the slow thawing of frozen emotions. They can now lead more normal lives, although the scars of fear and hatred may remain.

Others are not so fortunate. The strain of inner loneliness may be too great, and their strength may give way. They are then hospitalized for mental illness. Still others react violently against the society that they cannot understand. These are the habitual criminals who make headlines for crimes of violence, often showing irrational hatred.

Surprisingly enough there is another possibility, one that may seem completely unthinkable. They may turn to religion and may show extraordinary generosity in their faith and hope. It is interesting to note the spiritual development of those whose emotions were frozen by homes without love. They must begin with "naked faith," much like the faith described in the writings of St. John of the Cross. They do not know what hope and trust mean, so they cannot express these virtues in their relationship with God.

They know their pitiful needs, and they believe that God is good. Their prayer at first is for their most elementary wants: relief from loneliness and pain; some security; perhaps a good job. But their very handicaps make a life of prayer more natural to them. They seek God almost in desperation, but they do seek him.

Such prayer has its own inner momentum. As they grow in grace, they find the need for spiritual guidance. They associate with other devout souls and discover a kindness that they rarely met before.

58

As their emotions become more normal, they can now practice with assurance virtues that before carried no inner meaning to them. Love of God and neighbor become emotional realities, and not merely decisions of the will, taken in blind faith with neither intellectual understanding nor emotional reaction. Of course, from the viewpoint of merit, these earlier decisions were most pleasing to God. Nevertheless, it is usually better to base a life of virtue upon the foundation of a well developed and fully matured human personality.

Perhaps the work of winning such souls back to normal feelings of trust and love should be primarily the work of religious and religiously inspired laymen and laywomen who are willing to give disinterested, parental love to these afflicted souls. There are psychiatrists and social workers who have sensed these needs and met them. But the time and expense of such professional treatment are usually prohibitive.

In addition, persons whose emotions are frozen may rebel against professional treatment, unless the doctor or social worker first impresses them as a person of great kindness and infinite patience. Many of these patients become highly disturbed at probing questions and efforts to uncover repressed emotional injuries. They insist, and here our function is to report and not make psychological judgments, that they do not need insight, but rather understanding and disinterested love. Many of them are highly intelligent and appear to understand their own problem quite clearly.

They assert strongly that the love they need must be completely disinterested, the equivalent of the love given by a normal parent or brother or sister. If the helping person appears to have a selfish interest (even a quite legitimate one, such as the payment of a professional fee), barriers of distrust and fear are likely to arise. Strong religious motivation on the part of the person helping should give his compassionate love the quality that these should seek.

One such soul expressed the needs of the lonely quite well: These sufferers are usually unable to sustain "help" in the usual way. The best approach is the same one uses with a frightened puppy. You love them, notice them, encourage them (gently), don't worry about or fear them, don't approach them to help. Love them purely and detachedly, need their love in return, see the good that is in them and be prepared to remark about it openly once in a while, without condescension, but rather in honest appreciation.

They also need to know what about them is normal and good, not what is abnormal or bad, which is no help. Never confront them or talk down or analyze them. Share yourself with them. Never put them in a position to lie to you because, once they do, they may not be able to face you again. Do not expect to know more about them than they do—humbly expect the truth, and gradually you will get it. Share their cross and you will gradually understand them.

How can this approach of Bethany be used to help the many thousands who face the lifelong problem of complete inner loneliness? How can these victims of unhappy and unloving homes be taught to trust and love, and thus lead a more normal life? I raise these questions about a situation that many of us completely overlook. We may have met scores of persons afflicted with frozen emotions, without realizing why they are shy, retiring, and different. The experience of Bethany shows that religiously inspired love and compassion can bring hope to some, at least, who have had this problem. But the work of Bethany is quite specialized. It can indicate an approach, but the problem is how to use this approach more widely.

Helping the Unloved

When the chapter on "Love and the Fearful" was first published as a newspaper article,* it brought an outpouring of mail never before approached in the more than twenty years that I have been writing in national publications. Clearly it touched on a subject that was supremely important to thousands of lonely and anguished souls. Many writers said that this was the first article they had seen on the subject. They had seen much on mental illness, alcoholism, and nervous tension, but nothing on frozen emotions.

A common reaction was "How did you know?" "I thought no one else in the world understood my problem." Many writers explained the origin of their difficulties. Without exception, they spoke of a childhood without love. Perhaps their parents were constantly quarrelling. One parent might be an alcoholic. Some of the lonely ones were reared in orphan homes. Some were sent from one relative to another, or to a succession of foster

---

* *Our Sunday Visitor,* January 15, 1961.

homes. Lack of love might take the form of open abuse, but occasionally it was more subtle as "spoiled" children received all they wanted, except the one thing necessary, true parental love.

There were excellent analyses of the problem. For example: "People deprived of love view the world as a vicious battleground and humanity as their opponents. . . . Each setback in life is another brick in the vicious pyramid and each misunderstanding leads them to confirm their opinion that he who grabs, gets. . . . They are like cornered animals who lash out at everything in sight, so great is their fear of reopening or adding to the scars of their personalities."

"It is likened to a living death. They die because they cannot share as they are dying to share. Love is the most overwhelming force of all and, as you know, turned aside from its natural outlet, it degenerates into hate and fear. . . . Whenever they let down the guard, someone comes along to take another slice at their already dangerous state of insecurity. This is a fertile breeding ground for fear."

One surprise was the large number of letters from alcoholics and former mental patients. "Do you know, in your description of the lonely ones, you gave a perfect description of what ails the alcoholic?" It is also evident that the mentally ill often feel lonely and unloved. Quite a few former mental patients wrote that their home background was similar to that described in the earlier article. A doctor in a psychiatric clinic noted: "Your concepts are particularly appreciated because I have been using an almost identical approach to understanding the origin and possible cure of psychoneurotic and psychotic people who seek my help." Many cured mental patients mentioned the kindness of the doctors as a major factor in their recovery.

Beyond doubt, these correspondents consider the lack of love as a major factor in causing a wide variety of personality disorders and emotional illnesses. They likewise attribute great value to compassion and love shown by the counselor or therapist.

Another interesting reaction was the widespread testimony on the usefulness of group therapy. The organizations mentioned most frequently were Recovery, Inc., Alcoholics Anonymous, and Divorcees Anonymous. Significantly, however, hardly any writers whose problem was frozen emotions, without other complications, endorsed these forms of group therapy. Some, as will be explained in the following chapter, were helped by membership in parish organizations and participation in their activities. For most, the deep loneliness that follows from inability to trust and love can be dispelled only by personal compassion and love, and not by group therapy.

This last statement is not meant to be a dogmatic assertion, but only a reflection of the letters received. When the American Group Psychotherapy Association met in New York in 1960, papers were presented that apparently took a contrary view. Particularly interesting was the report of S. R. Slavson, reporting a five-year study of groups of delinquents at Children's Village, Dobbs Ferry, New York. The problems he described would seem clearly to be those of hostile youngsters from homes without love. To be sure, however, we would need further data. Many who are rebellious and disturbed do not completely lack the ability to trust and love.

Without passing any judgment on the value of group therapy, it may be helpful to relate instances in which individual help was valuable. One writer warns of the attitudes to expect when a friendly counselor tries to be of assistance. "Fear generates this urge to destroy in one form or another, and destruction feeds hate, rebellion, and distrust. Be prepared to be treated in this manner. First, a common ground must be found whereby you can gain entrance. This may be anything—ideas, dislikes, methods of doing things, etc. When this is established you have a pathway to the soul, but remember the guard is always up." The writer goes on to warn against analyzing the person being helped. He should rather learn to feel with him.

How this is done is spelled out in another letter. "Don't discuss the plight of the one you are trying to help with others—priests, sisters, lay teachers, etc." This destroys confidence and makes the subject selfconscious. "Need is the important thing. If you cannot convince those you are trying to help that you need them too, it becomes just another case of their needing someone desperately but they will try to hide that need if it is not returned. Make your love a personal thing. It is small comfort to be told 'I love everyone' or 'We all need each other.' He wants you to love and need him as he loves and needs you." Finally, the room in which conferences are held must protect the privacy of the conversation.

A college counselor notes that fearful people have little self-confidence and feel that they are unworthy of help.

To help, "The three most important tools that I know of are: prayer, love, and praise. To pray for a person is to learn to love him and, by so doing, you will soon find things you like about this person, and you will be able to praise him for something. One must never give way to discouragement, for if you are the only one taking an interest in this unfortunate person and *you* give up, whom will he be able to depend on? It is the steady, constant, and nonexpecting love of the mother for a child that has to be shown to this fearful person, if you are to succeed."

"What I mean by 'nonexpecting' is that you will see this person make mistakes, and even *seem* to go backward, and yet you will not take him to task for it. It is hard work to help these fearful people, which is, no doubt, why little has been written on the subject, but if you have patience, compassion, and courage, you can do a great deal." "I have likened this process to caring for a plant, and making it bloom with sunshine, water, and loving words. . . . Prayer is the key word, I believe, with patience, love, and encouragement bestowed in generous doses."

Much can be done, says another correspondent, merely by being a good neighbor. "If you have a normal life . . . and become acquainted with a friend or relative who everybody else seems to think is not worth having around, just make up your mind to accept him the way he is. Extend to him an open invitation to join in your ordinary family life, whether it be putting up a clothesline, washing the car, or taking the children to the zoo or the movies. Treat him like a member of your family, not a guest. If he wants to do something for you in return for your hospitality, be glad to accept it. It is something that he feels he owes you for the feeling of belonging you have given him. Make your home a haven for him when he feels there is no place to go and no one else to care what happens to him."

Several have written to note how they brought love into a marriage, when one partner at first lacked the ability to love. Building up self-confidence was the first step in one case. "I told him how good he was and I praised his good qualities, not only to him, but to friends and relatives. . . . The change was very gradual, and some times he would go back to being hateful, but this happened less and less." In another situation: "the first thing that had to be established was his faith and trust in me. . . . It took years and it took patience. Mindful that he was an adult, not a child, he had to learn of his own volition that he loved me, albeit, he was being taught. His trust and his love had to be tested from time to time (not too light, not too strong). . . . His ego had to be bolstered—and deflated occasionally—just the right amount. It meant for me a *complete* subjugation of my own feelings, to the point of allowing good friends to be treated rudely, and often insulted."

It is obvious that this apostolate is not easy. "It takes almost Divine Love to help them, and not too many people are capable of that kind of love. . . . If they can find Him through some human relationship, someone who is capable of such divine love, then both the giver and the receiver will have fulfilled God's designs, and no telling how many may move because of these two." The writer goes on to mention a well known living spiritual writer whom she considers as one who has been so aided and now helps millions.

Because of the difficulties involved, some suggest a special form of religious society or secular institute to help both the mentally ill and those with personality disturbances. Several writers mentioned Father Edward Dowling, S.J., as a priest with extraordinary compassion toward such afflicted souls. Others spoke of priests of great kindness and patience, those who always encourage, those who never have a harsh word. (One here thinks of the exhortations to priests by Pope John XXIII.)

At the risk of oversimplification, the central theme of these letters is that love more than any other quality will heal the wounds of those who are unable to love or trust. But this love and compassion must be special, completely unselfish, infinitely patient and understanding. Those who have seen the healing work of such love, whether in the world or in the hidden apostolate of such religious as the Dominican Sisters of Bethany, begin to understand the fullness of Christ's mission. If we too could practice his love, the power of miracles would be ours. We might not raise the dead or heal the sick, but we would do what is much more important—heal an inner sickness and conquer an inner death for those to whom life seems to offer no hope and no mercy.

The Unloved Help Themselves

In the correspondence occasioned by "Love and the Fearful," there is a marked contrast between the number of letters noting what others may do to help and those telling what the victim can do for himself. There were scores of writers with useful suggestions for aiding the lonely. But only a very few told how the prisoner of frozen emotions can escape without outside aid. This excludes, of course, those who suggested group therapy. But the groups listed were formed to deal with other problems. It is not clear that they can help those with frozen emotions.

There was general agreement that the most important first step to be taken by those who lack love is to seek to deepen their practice of prayer and faith. "A kindly psychiatrist asked me if I believed in God. He told me that I must find something to believe in, because my sickness seemed to be that of the soul. The inner pain had become so intense and unrelenting by this time that I no longer wanted to live.

"Then one day I heard Bishop Sheen's voice on the radio. He said something about 'the love that waits for you.' A faint hope stirred. I listened. You see, Father Cronin, no one ever really wants to die to relieve this terribly unrelenting pain. They simply don't know the way out. Someone has to lead them. Although I knew nothing of Catholicism, I found the nearest Catholic Church. After my second lesson from the priest, I knew somehow that *this* was the *truth*."

This writer went through a deep spiritual experience. "The pain was gone. I felt happy and loved. . . . A faith so overwhelming that it cannot be described came to me. However, it was made very clear to me that this was a gift of which I was undeserving. It was given to me because of my great need and the generosity of God."

"The Blessed Mother is the answer to the whole problem, it seems to me. You have a Mother who is perfect, all loving, faithful, and trustworthy to offer to these people who never knew a mother's love. Let them test her. She never fails. . . . She will do all the lovely things they long for a mother to do. Give them a mother."

"In summing up, I would say from my own experience that the very best and most magnificent of human love cannot satisfy or ease one iota the pain of the loveless. It has to be the Divine love first, and after that all else follows in natural order."

Another writer suggests that the person search for a good regular confessor and spiritual director. He must have the same temperament and outlook. He also must be patient and willing to give a great deal of time and adequate spiritual direction. Unfortunately, according to quite a few correspondents, this advice is not easy to follow. They say that few priests have the time and inclination for really adequate spiritual direction. Nor do many have the empathy and insight needed to understand and treat this problem.

The replies that touched on spiritual matters often revealed souls of extraordinary spiritual depth. One is given the feeling that proper acceptance of the sufferings involved in this deep-rooted loneliness has produced uncanonized saints. Many seem to have a surer touch and sounder perception than is found in the average published article on spiritual subjects.

In connection with the approach of faith and divine love, certain cautions must be noted. One must not expect overnight miraculous cures. The growth in faith and trust normally takes many years. Moreover, as was noted in the original article, there comes a stage when God provides unselfish human love to guide the soul that is finding its way in the new world of love and trust.

On the other hand, it would be wrong to discount this approach on the grounds that it is an improper use of supernatural means. Writers on pastoral counseling wisely advise the clergy not to rely exclusively on spiritual aids for problems that call for medical care. This is sound advice for persons afflicted with mental illness and related disorders that demand professional medical help. Even here, it is widely conceded that a sound and intense spiritual life strongly supplements the work of the therapist.

But the problem of souls whose emotions were frozen by homes without love is not one of mental illness, according to the correspondence received, including letters from the medical and social-work professions. While these persons suffer from strong fears and even hostility, this is a normal reaction to the background factors and experiences that caused their insecurity and emotional blockage. Their perception of reality is unclouded. They suffer only from an inability to respond adequately. The need is not for correct insight—this they already have—but for a healing love that will awaken their own latent abilities to trust and love.

Even with the assurance that comes through faith and the love of God, there remains the long struggle of adjusting to normal social life. Here one must get from prayer the strength to learn to meet people. "I do remember that I used to beg God and Our Lady for charity, although I had no concept of what charity was, and for a relief from the terror of being around people. I was horribly with-drawn until I went to work for ———. Then I was in an office full of the most wonderful people.

"My job there brought me necessarily in contact with everyone. I learned a lot of tact and diplomacy—that one always thanks someone for doing something correctly even if it is his job; that one always smiles and requests what you have a right to, with deference and without being demanding; how to overlook the trivial, to encourage, and to compromise with other people's wishes where it could be done. Needless to say I had to learn the hard way, but my job depended on it.

"Also, I took a great deal of pride that people would smile at me and talk with me when I came into their offices, which was often. I needed attention and approval, and this was one way to get it. I got teased soundly all over the building. I'd never been able to take teasing before, but theirs was so jolly and benevolent that I grew to thrive on it.

"Outside the job? I had to go to the store, ride buses, etc. I used to suffer torment around strangers. I was always afraid that the strain would show in my expression and this added to my fear. But I could not bear to have people angry with me and I loved to see people smile, so I would try to smile at them—the checkers in the grocery store, etc. I could not force social contacts, but I used to force myself, when I was riding buses, to look out the window at people as they went by. I think it is enough to require only a minimum of *necessary* contacts, but to do these charitably, *as best one can with regard to the needs of the other people involved.*"

She notes that smiling at neighbors and fellow workers, and showing interest when they are talking, makes them like a person. There remains the fear that they will get to know her and not like her. But she must convince herself that she is no worse than they are. She must never pry into their affairs, or reveal the secrets of her heart to someone she does not trust implicitly. And finally, she must neither expect perfection from them or from herself. People know our exterior faults, but rarely know our inner troubles. Often the need to be loved is satisfied only after the need to give love is satisfied.

"This is not complete, certainly. . . . without prayer, much of it crying on God's shoulder, my efforts would have broken me. I was in agony all the time as it was."

Other writers suggest getting into some kind of lay apostolic action group, preferably spiritually accented ones. Among the groups mentioned were the Legion of Mary, the Confraternity of Christian Doctrine (especially the Helpers' Committee), the St. Vincent de Paul Society, the Christian Family Movement, and the Young Christian Workers.

"Through C.F.M. I learned to approach my neighbors as a duty. Now I do it as a pleasure." "In my own estimation, I would say that the YCW meetings straightened me out. For one thing, we developed a Christian attitude toward life and its many problems . . . we were trained to share our faith by helping others. Right there is where I think my problem of not feeling loved was solved."

"Getting to know Christ through the Y.C.W. convinced me that He loved me and cared about my future. For the first time in my life, I felt a security and self-confidence I had never experienced before. Since being loved and being needed go hand in hand, Catholic action was the solution. My two doctors were amazed when they saw me two or three months after I was in Y.C.W. . . . The one doctor just sat and shook his head and said he couldn't believe I was the same person." She notes that this technique worked equally well with another person who was at the point of breaking down.

Here again, a word of caution is in order. One does not cure in a few months or a year a disorder that has built up over ten or twenty years. Even when there may be every surface appearance of drastic change, emotional scars remain. But the improvement can be sufficient to permit normal living, including marriage and the performance of most types of work.

Among the miscellaneous suggestions was recreation of some sort that the person enjoys, whether this be physically active or passive. Some have seen this affliction in saints or other well known persons. Those mentioned included St. Thérèse of Lisieux, St. Benedict Joseph Labre, Matt Talbott, and Francis Thompson. Writings recommended were: The works of Thomas Merton; De Lehen, *The Way of Interior Peace;* Barta, *The Moral Theory of Human Behavior;* and Rev. Narciso Irala, *Achieving Peace of Heart.*

It is my hope that these suggestions, compiled from hundreds of letters, will bring hope to those who have had no hope, and may give light to those who have lived in the darkness of inner loneliness. They can find trust and love, from the love of God and the compassion of those whose lives reflect this divine love.

IV

The Catholic Image in Race Relations

Are These Also Our Brothers?

The sensitive Christian, seeking to mold society in accord with the truths of the Gospel, must confront the race problem. If he lives in the South, the immediate issue is integration in the schools. If he lives in the North, his concern centers about housing and jobs for minority groups. But wherever he lives, the really critical problem, if he is white, is that of attitude toward his Negro brothers in Christ.

There should be no problem of attitude. In the words of the American bishops, "Our Christian Faith is of its nature universal. It knows not the distinction of race, color, or nationhood. . . . The love of Christ, and the love of the Christian, knows no bounds." Our Faith teaches that Christ died for all men, that we are brothers under an eternal Father, that we are all called to be members of Christ's Mystical Body, the Church.

The Gospels, the epistles, the solemn statements of Pope Pius XII and Pope John XXIII—all affirm the truth of the unity of the human race. These popes, the bishops of the United States, and the bishops of South Africa have explicitly affirmed that racism is evil and un-Christian. Our bishops are quite emphatic that enforced legal segregation "by its very nature imposes a stigma of inferiority

74

upon the segregated people." For this reason, and because of the evil fruits of segregation, they conclude that enforced segregation cannot be reconciled with the Christian view of our fellow man.

To many white Catholics these are "hard sayings." It is well known that certain among us have explicitly rejected the Church's teaching on this subject. Others remain silent, but they are hurt and puzzled. They cannot reconcile the views of the Church with attitudes that they have held since childhood. Some say that the popes and the bishops do not understand the problem. They do not have to live with it.

This reaction is not new. When our Lord first preached the doctrine of the Eucharist, some found it hard to believe and followed him no longer. God's law on the permanence of marriage can be a grievous burden to the separated Catholic. There are some who cannot take it, and remarry, thus losing access to the sacraments. Those who would follow a crucified Savior must be prepared to carry their own crosses. Some rebel.

Confronted with such problems, a kindly pastor of souls does not aggravate the situation by seeking to impose blind obedience. He tries to nourish the flickering flame of good will by sympathetic explanation of the will of God. He shows understanding of the anguish felt by the troubled soul. While he cannot compromise on God's law, he can make every effort to secure willing acceptance rather than cold and enforced obedience.

Catholics should take this same pastoral attitude when racial problems are discussed. They should seek to understand the complexity of the situation, its personal and historical roots, and the difficulties involved in modifying lifelong convictions or even prejudices.

Generally speaking, the Catholic who balks at racial equality is not ill disposed toward the Negro as a person. On the contrary, he is probably kind in his personal contacts. He is a good employer. He may be most helpful when sickness or tragedy strikes a Negro family that he knows. He can say with sincere conviction that his attitude is one of Christian charity.

But, for various reasons, he balks at the concept of equality. He will gladly offer the kindness of a gracious superior toward an inferior. But he rejects the parity implied in a nonsegregated society. He asserts that this is unrealistic, since the Negroes he knows are culturally inferior to whites. He considers the Negro community to be demoralized. He does not want this contagion to affect his children and his neighborhood. Let the Negro progress in education, in economic status, and in culture, but let him do this separately. Perhaps when this process is completed, the question of equality can then be discussed realistically.

The fallacy—and the tragedy—in this thinking is that the process may never be completed in a segregated society. When an entire social structure stigmatizes a race as inferior, it is virtually impossible for that race to rise to higher levels. There are many reasons why this is so. The most fundamental is that it is difficult to acquire a sense of human dignity when one is being treated constantly as less than fully human. When rights are being denied to a Negro community, how can it be expected to assert these same rights in its own internal affairs?

The segregationist argues that among Negroes there is little respect for property, for sexual continence, or even for human life. And he will cite statistics to prove his point. But he fails to see that the vices of certain Negroes are direct products of a segregated society. If some steal, or are incontinent, or are violent in venting their anger, are they acting differently from the way whites would act under similar conditions? That question can be answered by reading accounts of behavior in concentration camps and prisoner-of-war camps. Far too many products of our so-called superior white culture succumb when treated barbarously.

A common stereotype of the Negro is that he is shiftless and lazy. Yet when some white Americans visit their ancestral lands, they are often shocked to find that their compatriots are often very unprogressive. If they are understanding, they may realize that poverty of soil and lack of opportunity may kill initiative. Poor diet and elementary medical care may so weaken bodies that hard work is almost impossible.

Many Negroes suffer from similar disabilities. Their education is inferior or even nonexistent. Even where opportunity for education exists, there may be no incentive to accept it. The educated Negro who cannot find a job in which he can use his talents suffers even more than the Negro who gave up early. He is condemned to frustration and rebellion.

Thus the vicious and demoralizing circle goes on. Escape from it is extraordinarily difficult. The ambitious Negro farm boy in the South may find a little more opportunity in the city, but this is counterbalanced by crowded slum conditions. If he moves to a Northern city, again his fate may be slums and inferior jobs. He is often segregated factually, if not legally. He may not face contempt, but he often faces indifference.

There are two ways to break this vicious circle. One is to fight one's way out by using every legal and economic weapon available for the purpose of securing justice. Court actions can be taken to strike down laws imposing segregation. Boycotts can win fair treatment in buses. Laws and persuasion can break down discrimination in jobs.

The path of justice under law is frequently used today. It is thoroughly legitimate, but it suffers from certain limitations. It tends to enhance frictions and increase prejudice. Certainly its use in the South, at least in the short range, has caused racial relations to deteriorate. The same in true in some Northern cities, especially where housing is involved.

These by-products can be avoided if justice is complemented by Christian love of neighbor. As Pope Pius XI observed, "justice alone can never bring about union of minds and hearts." Without this bond of charity, "the best of regulations can come to naught, as we have learned by too frequent experience." The race problem will be solved by the moral conscience of the American people, and not by legal action alone.

Before we consider any question of techniques or methods, we must face up to one basic problem of attitude. We must ask ourselves one critical question: Are we as Christians willing and eager to help our fellow man who is of a different race? Let us for the moment leave aside questions of integration or segregation, of cultural inferiority or superiority. The fundamental issue is our willingness to help our Negro brethren to live a better life, both spiritually and materially.

If we want them to be better off, much better off, than they are today, then we are viewing the problem with a Christian attitude. If we are willing to do something personally, as our opportunities permit, we are ready to put this Christian attitude into practice. At this stage the biggest hurdle in the struggle toward fair treatment of a different race has been passed.

The Christian who makes this affirmation is like the person who is seeking to be generous in the service of God. The first offer of love and total dedication to the Lord is a tremendous step. It is not final or irrevocable. There can be failures and moments of discouragement. But such a soul is on the right path.

It is in this spirit that we must face the race problem. We must stand on Calvary and there realize that Christ is dying for all mankind. If our hearts can absorb something of this love, our minds can then take up the question of methods and techniques. These points will be discussed in the chapter to follow.

Approaches to Racial Justice

The Catholic who wants to help his Negro brethren has the right moral attitude. He is not poisoned by the thoroughly un-Christian virus of hatred and racism. But good will needs to be translated into intelligent and effective action. This will be a complex and long drawn-out process. But it is essential if America is to be a morally healthy nation.

It would be ideal if we could approach this problem with the same attitudes and insights as those possessed by the Apostles and the saints. They learned from our Savior the divine art of seeing the potential for good in those who seem most removed from our normal Christian customs and ideals. The early Christians worked among the slaves of ancient Rome. St. Peter Claver worked with the Negro slaves of modern times. The healing Christian love of these saints helped overcome the degrading and brutalizing surroundings of these unfortunates and lifted them to a life of faith and grace.

The ability to see the true human dignity of every person, no matter how sparse his education or how repulsive his surroundings, is a truly apostolic gift. It is life-giving and creative. It can help unfortunate minority groups, and slum-dwellers everywhere, to get the will and the opportunity to break out of the demoralizing vicious circle that presently confines some of them.

If this apostolic insight is hard to come by—and we should pray that God may give it to us—we can at least try to get the basic intellectual convictions needed to promote racial justice and harmony. First among these is the conviction that enforced segregation, whether by law or by other pressures, is essentially degrading and unjust. Its very existence puts a label of inferiority upon its victims. So long as we deny a race moral equality, we cannot really help them to advance culturally and economically.

Moral equality is based on the dignity of the human

person as a child of God. It exists no matter how great differences may be in language, customs or culture. Once it is recognized, then we can proceed to remove the obstacles that currently prevent most Negroes from advancing in education, economic status, and acceptance of community customs and moral standards.

Next come consistent efforts to secure three basic rights that should be given to every American citizen: rights to education, to job opportunity, and to equal justice under law. In some areas of the United States, we might add a fourth basic right: the right to secure decent housing in wholesome surroundings. These rights are basic since, where they are denied, progress becomes almost impossible.

Education is a difficult problem for most of our Negro youth. Under segregated conditions it was inferior in quality. The lack of job opportunity sapped incentive and discouraged initiative. Poor home conditions made for an added burden. There were difficulties in finding a time and place for study. When the parents themselves were almost illiterate, their children often lacked proper guidance and encouragement.

Given these conditions, there will be problems in integrated schools. Those who want to go back to segregation can find plenty of excuse for opposing and hampering the change to integrated schooling. It is essential that our white students, with the encouragement of their parents, realize that the transitional period will be difficult for both races. Patience and good will are necessary to achieve the breakthrough in regard to the vicious circle hitherto prevailing.

We must remember that the Negro child who seeks a good education today is making an act of faith in regard to job opportunities tomorrow. It would be heartbreaking if he were to acquire skills or business or professional knowledge and then be unable to use these abilities in earning his livelihood. Accordingly an essential element in the breakthrough of minority groups is the availability of work without discrimination on any basis other than ability.

This has been obtained in some states and cities by laws that enforce fair-employment practices. Most of the gains achieved this way are secured by persuasion and conciliation rather than compulsion. These techniques are also used by the President's Committee on Equal Employment Opportunity in regard to employers who have substantial federal contracts.

Again the right to vote and to equal justice under law is basic. This is a fundamental civil right. Without it, we can hardly speak of a group as being really citizens. Moreover, it is of the greatest tactical importance. When minority groups can vote in sizable numbers, they are in a far better position to secure their other rights.

Finally, we can list the right to housing opportunity as normally essential for decent family life. Discrimination in housing inflicts a twofold hurt: the insult that is inseparable from discrimination; and the damage to the family that often results from resultant crowding into subhuman slums. It should hurt us as Christians to see any family forced to live in overcrowded and unwholesome conditions. But this is a greater injustice when the family is able and willing to pay for good housing.

Once progress is made in these vital areas, the others usually take care of themselves. Among the others are access without discrimination to tax-supported services and facilities and access to private facilities that others can patronize if they are willing to pay the price and follow the rules. Examples would be public libraries and parks, and private stores, hotels, restaurants, theaters, and bus services.

No comment is offered here on social relations since these are not normally considered matters of right and justice. In this area one can pick companions according to standards appropriate in the circumstances. A choral group has a right to test the voices of prospective members. A private golf club may seek compatible members. Even here we should be sensitive to sins against charity, if we make race by itself a basis of exclusion.

The bugaboo of intermarriage hardly needs mention. In our country marriage is a matter of consent between adults, or children with parental consent. No one is forced to marry anyone else. Indeed, a forced marriage is invalid by both civil and canon law. The wisdom of racial intermarriage is strictly a matter to be decided by the parties contemplating such marriage.

Catholics seeking to participate in community programs for interracial justice will hear all types of objections to such programs. They will range from difficulties found in integrated schools to property deterioration caused by "blockbusting." It would take too long to list and answer all the arguments that can be raised. Those who are interested will find that these difficulties have been met successfully in various parts of the country.

Indeed, once good will is available, one of the greatest needs is to learn experiences and techniques from other areas and groups that have overcome the major problems. There is no point in repeating errors that have been corrected elsewhere. For example, Louisville and Nashville could be good examples of quiet school integration. There are similar examples in regard to job opportunities and housing.

In this connection, much can be said for the suggestion of committees of conciliation in various major areas of the country. If such committees could co-ordinate activities and pool experiences, work could proceed much more rapidly and effectively. Had such approaches been attempted after the Supreme Court decision of 1954, much grief could have been avoided. Now, unfortunately, the issue is too often one of prestige and pride, rather than of justice and charity.

Because conditions have deteriorated in the last several years, the work of the racial apostolate is by no means easy today. Now more than ever there is need of dedicated souls, willing to sacrifice—and sacrifice greatly—for love of God and their fellow man.

It may be that the real secret of the message of Fatima may be found in these areas of personal sacrifice. The Virgin Mary preached prayer, penance, and the renewal of a Christian life. If Christians are willing to pray and sacrifice to help their unfortunate neighbor here at home, the effect would be twofold. First, an example that would have repercussions throughout the world and offset Communist propaganda directed against the Christian West. Secondly, and even more important, a source of the greatest graces and blessings from heaven. The message of Fatima was a promise, if we lived our faith, of the conversion, not the destruction of Russia.

Religion and Race

The record of church and synagogue in the area of interracial justice has been mixed. On the one hand, the religious conscience has always been uneasy in the face of racial discrimination. Religious leaders were among the strongest fighters against slavery. The Negro church is the prime source of inspiration and encouragement for those who are trying to break the patterns of forced segregation. Most of our major religious bodies have made statements on racial justice, none more eloquent or forthright than that of our own bishops in 1958.

Yet it can also be said that organized religion has lagged in its duty of fighting racial discrimination. To mention failures within the Catholic Church, we have been much slower in challenging community customs in race relations than we have been in fighting other moral evils. We have had segregated Church institutions, not only in the Deep South, but also in border states and even in Northern areas. Catholic interracial councils came into being a little over thirty years ago. Even Catholics in the social action field had a tendency, all too often, to consider interracial work a special apostolate.

It has been said that "eleven o'clock Sunday morning is the most segregated hour in the United States." Yet priests, rabbis, and ministers have often made heroic sacrifices for the cause of racial justice. Special tribute must be paid to Protestant ministers, since many of them lost their pulpits because of their courageous struggle for Negro rights. Even now I can see the tense, whitened face of a Southern Catholic bishop, as he participated in the final editorial work on the 1958 Bishops' Statement on Discrimination and the Christian Conscience. He anticipated that the Statement would cause serious problems in his diocese, but he bravely co-operated in helping fashion a document that his conscience declared to be right and necessary.

However one interprets the past in terms of religious achievement in interracial matters, there can be little question that the present stand of church and synagogue is clear and unequivocal. This was demonstrated in 1963 by the history-making National Conference on Religion and Race. The statistics alone are impressive. Nearly 70 national religious bodies participated. There were about 700 delegates, plus an approximate 500 observers from the Chicago area. One of the most faithful delegates in attendance was the Cardinal Archbishop of Chicago. Over 20 other Catholic archbishops and bishops participated, in spite of all the pressures caused by their long absence from their sees while attending Vatican Council II.

Two features of this Conference contributed to its unique quality. One was the clear and unanimous affirmation that organized religion in the United States must place its resources in the struggle for the recognition of the God-given dignity of all men, regardless of race. The second was the fact that, for the first time in our history, the major religious groups in our nation met at the highest level for common action in a cause sanctioned by religion and morality, and concerned with the common social good.

The convening organizations were the National Council of the Churches of Christ, the Synagogue Council of America, and the National Catholic Welfare Conference. The positions of honor reflected the religious and racial composition of the Conference. Its Chairman was Protestant and Negro. Vice Chairmen were a Catholic Archbishop, an Orthodox Bishop, a Jewish Rabbi, and a Protestant Bishop who was also a Negro. The one speaker to receive a standing ovation before and after his talk was the Reverend Martin Luther King.

From an ecumenical viewpoint, the Conference taught the lesson that religious groups work best together when they are challenged by a vital common cause. In the scores of planning sessions that led to the Conference, there was no artificial allocation of posts of honor, no jockeying for prestige, no effort to push the achievements and claims of any religious body. If some thought that the Conference underplayed the good work already done by religious America, we can rejoice that the delegates were much more concerned with emphasizing duties and opportunities than with seeking any credit for past performance.

Those who feared that the Conference would be merely a sounding board for pious platitudes were happily convinced of their error. The quiet determination of the delegates at the Conference was matched by their equal zeal to organize interreligious, interracial activities in their own communities. It was fitting that the host city of Chicago should take the leadership in the continuing work of justice and charity, but dozens of other cities are quietly seeking to do as well. The tremendous ecumenical push resulting from the opening session of Vatican Council II has been reinforced by the unprecedented co-operative effort of the National Conference on Religion and Race.

There were many practical conclusions reached at the Conference. Among the most important was the common conviction that religious bodies should co-operate closely in interracial work. This was stated at the opening night by the Cardinal Archbishop of Chicago, in a major address to the Conference. It was reinforced by the Archbishop of Milwaukee, who was one of the three Convenors of the Conference, acting in his capacity as Chairman of the Social Action Department, N.C.W.C. Protestant, Orthodox, and Jewish spokesmen equally endorsed this position. It was officially approved by the National Council of Churches in its General Board meeting in the spring of 1963.

The delegates expressed the conviction that religion has a unique place in the quest for full equality for all Americans. One can forbid discrimination by law, but only religion can impel men to put aside prejudice and accept all men as brothers under the fatherhood of God. The quest for justice, necessary as it is, can be incomplete in the absence of religiously inspired love of neighbor. Religious America should take its part in the fight for the rights of minorities, but it should also keep in mind its unique role in its ministry of reconciliation.

It is fitting that organized religion begin by cleaning its own house. This requires that its members be taught to infuse in their lives the full implications of the faith they profess. There should be no segregation in church and synagogue, and in institutions under religious control. Hospitals, homes for the aged, and camps should be open to all, regardless of race. Employment practices should be exemplary. While these internal reforms are the primary responsibility of individual religious bodies, it may often be helpful to co-ordinate official announcements. Thus, the stronger churches can carry the weaker, and the true nature of our beliefs will be made manifest to all.

Religious groups should consider their moral obligations in such matters as letting of construction contracts or purchasing for their institutions. In the past, many groups felt it their duty to aid labor organization by favoring union labor in construction and purchasing. The need of Negro workers for equal employment opportunity is so great today that we can hardly be indifferent to it in using our funds. We can favor contractors and suppliers who consistently afford to minority groups, especially Negroes, opportunities to obtain jobs and promotions in terms of their abilities alone. Since the federal government and many states and cities are similarly concerned, the full integration of the Negro into our economic society should not be long delayed.

Religion can play an important role in achieving open occupancy of housing within a community. When clergy and religiously inspired laity take the leadership in welcoming new neighbors of another race, existing ghettoes will disappear and the vicious consequences of overcrowding can be prevented. Interestingly enough, virtue in this regard can pay off economically. Mass racial movements in a city tend to disrupt churches, schools, and synagogues.

If Negroes, and other minorities, can move freely within a city and its suburbs, there is less danger that religious institutions may be left stranded as parishioners or congregants move out.

Cardinal Meyer singled out as a special need the securing of employment for Negro youth. The unemployment rate among school drop-outs is very high. Lack of incentive and opportunity turn many in the direction of crime. Unquestionably the crime rate is high in slums, and discrimination in housing and jobs has forced Negroes to live in slums. This environment creates an additional handicap to their acceptance in our society. A much more fruitful and honest approach, as Archbishop Shehan pointed out in his magnificent Lenten Pastoral Letter of 1963, is to face the basic causes of crime and delinquency. Racial discrimination ranks high among these causes.

One final warning was given to Conference delegates, as they prepared to seek a program of interreligious, interracial action. It is vital that white congregations speak together *with* their Negro brethren, and not merely preach *to* Negroes or *for* Negroes. An interreligious program that is not sensitive on this point may be badly handicapped as a result of previous policies of discrimination. A central church body in a given city may be exclusively white in terms of effective membership. Any organizing committee for religious interracial action must seek out Negro leadership from the beginning as full participants in any program.

This may not be as easy as it seems, as the planners for the National Conference on Religion and Race discovered. Negroes are so fearful of token offers of participation that they often hold back. Past rebuffs make them suspicious and somewhat aloof. Hence, to use the Gospel phrase, they must be "compelled to enter." They should know that they are fully welcome and that their views will be sought and treated with the utmost respect. Unless they can come in as full partners, they will remain hesitant and unco-operative.

While America observes the centenary of the Emancipation Proclamation, there is the uneasy conviction that the work of racial justice must still be classed as unfinished business. Yet tremendous progress has been made since the beginning of World War II. If religion in America can maintain and increase the momentum developed at the National Conference on Religion and Race, it may soon merit the plaudit "Well done, faithful servant of the eternal Father."

V

The Catholic Image and Church Unity

Our Separated Brethren

The present Ecumenical Council has excited considerable interest in the problem of Church unity. Yet it is well to remember that current endeavors are but the climax of movements that have continued for decades and even centuries. We have an annual Church Unity Octave. Doctrinal discussions among the Churches have been common, especially in Europe. Orthodox, Lutheran, and Anglican groups have been particularly interested in unity.

Here we shall not enter into the area of high-level discussions on doctrine. This is a field for experts. But everyone should be interested in religious diversity as a social problem. Every Catholic parent knows the difficulties faced in explaining to children why their playground or school companions go to a different church or to no church at all.

It is not easy to deal with religious diversity without creating prejudice or personal antagonisms. In the first place, any Church that believes it is the unique custodian of divine revelation must hold that conflicting faiths are wrong. Catholics, Orthodox, Lutherans, and Orthodox Jews are certainly in this position. Other Protestant groups than those named may so believe, or at least they may hold that one or more different faiths (usually Catholic and Jewish) are in error.

Even if history did not teach the lesson, simple logic would warn us of the social tensions inherent in such a situation. Religion is, or should be, a vital factor in the lives of believers. When people differ on deeply held and emotionally charged principles, some tension is inevitable and conflict is not easily avoided. Friendships have been broken on lesser issues, such as politics, labor-union policy, or the Cold War.

History bears out this analysis. Europe has had its religious wars. The United States has had persecutions, less bloody but scarcely less bitter. Prejudice and bigotry exist in our nation today, sometimes openly, sometimes in a concealed manner. Often the victims of one type of prejudice may be perpetrators of another. Groups that profess to be free of religious bigotry may attack a Church for its social or political policies. Hence the well known phrase: "Anti-Catholicism is the antisemitism of the liberal."

While many persons deplore religious tension, it is not always easy to come up with satisfactory means for lessening or avoiding it. Some seek to solve the problem by preaching religious indifferentism. They say that "all religions are equally good." "We all seek the same goal, but by different means." "Religion is a matter of taste, so why quarrel over it?"

Such approaches may be well meaning. Yet, objectively speaking, they are insulting to a believer in revealed religion. Such a believer has no choice in his faith. It was given to him by God, and his duty is to believe and prac-

tice, not to pick and choose among doctrines and practices. Only those who hold that divine revelation was
given in a general manner, with each individual guided by
God to choose according to his needs, can consistently
be indifferent to differing beliefs.

Much of the religious world today is not satisfied with
indifferentism. It is difficult, almost impossible, to have
a Church without a body of belief. If this belief is held
as both true and divinely revealed, one can hardly accept
conflicting faiths as equally true. Where there is little or
no conflict, one can treat a differing faith as incomplete.
The Orthodox might so regard the Lutherans. But when
tenets contradict one another, one or both must be false.

In practice, of course, expressions of indifferentism are
often merely social conventions. They are used as a polite
way to say: Let us not discuss religion. But, even when
used in this fashion, they may be quite inadequate. Strong
religious differences are facts that will not vanish merely
because we are polite in mixed gatherings. They must be
faced head-on if they are to be resolved.

One way of doing this is to have public discussions
among clergy or informed laity of differing faiths, usually
on a tripartite basis—Catholic, Protestant, and Jewish.
These discussions may deal with religious questions, or
they may simply present various approaches to a social
problem. For example, a priest, minister, and rabbi may
discuss the racial question. They may even talk about
religious tolerance.

The author has participated in a number of such public
meetings, without any impression that they accomplished
much. They seemed too superficial, especially when the

subject was tolerance, to change many convictions or to eradicate prejudices. Incidental good was done when an audience got its first direct contact with a representative of a minority faith. But basic issues were rarely touched.

A somewhat deeper approach is the Springfield Plan, used in many schools. The purpose of this method is to give students an objective and fair understanding of major beliefs and practices of Catholics, Protestants, and Jews. Such a technique, when used competently, can dispel prejudices based on misunderstandings. But it is not likely to remove dislikes that have solid foundations. For example, if a Protestant dislikes Catholics because of their principles on divorce or birth control, a fair explanation of Catholic doctrine given in a public school could hardly touch the source of the antipathy.

Just to make the problem more complicated, it is not always easy to get to the real roots of religious tension. Suppose that a non-Catholic were to believe that a life of celibacy is impossible for a normal person. He would then have to hold that priests and nuns are either abnormal or that they are hypocrites. Since charges of this nature are rather crude, he is likely—consciously or unconsciously—to rationalize his views by seeking other objections.

The reverse of this situation also occurs. A minority religious group may not like to face up to the real roots of the opposition that may exist in a community. Hence it ascribes the dislike to some form of religious bigotry. Let us suppose, for instance, that Catholics in a given parish were acting in a rather high-handed fashion. The rest of the community may consider them arrogant and react accordingly. Arrogant Catholics would hardly own up to the fact. They are far more likely to consider the hostility they sense as mere bigotry.

Unfortunately, the two situations just considered are not easily treated. In the first place, they may not be recognized by the parties concerned. It is commonly observed by students of psychology that roots of hostility are often hidden and may be most difficult to discover. Hence any discussion of differences that does not probe to the real causes is merely treating symptoms. Understandably it will not accomplish much.

A second difficulty in these cases is the fact that people may be unwilling to discuss them even when they know the causes of hostility. How would one discuss clerical celibacy in a prejudiced backwater community that had never seen a priest? This would be all the more difficult if this community had been fed the lurid stories that certain bigoted groups distribute.

It may be possible to discuss differences on one level, but not on another. In recent years, for example, the Fund for the Republic has sponsored high-level, no-holds-barred, discussions of religious differences. The meetings were not public, and participants were men of wide experience and sophistication in matters of intergroup contacts.

Such an experienced assembly could discuss issues frankly and with a minimum of emotion. Perhaps the question may be raised of using political means to achieve religious ends. A member of the group may distinguish between areas of public morals, where a Church has a right and often a duty to speak out, and the seeking of special favors or the promoting of doctrines specific to a particular religious faith by means of public facilities.

A distinction of this nature may weed out a certain number of objections. Thus, if Protestants consider legalized gambling to be immoral, and Catholics do not, it can at least be conceded that both have the right to urge their points of view. The decision in such cases must be made by the electorate on the basis of the arguments offered and its judgment of how a vote will affect the public welfare.

Delicate problems arise when a minority religious group complains about matters of public policy influenced by the religious views of a majority. A Sunday closing law for stores may be desired by the dominant Christian community. Some Jewish groups and minor Protestant sects may oppose it, since Saturday is their day of worship. Does the freedom of worship guaranteed to minorities extend to such indirect areas of public policy?

Questions of this nature are not readily answered, even in dispassionate, high-level discussions. They could lead to considerable tensions on a local level, where personalities and feelings are likely to enter into any debate. Yet issues of this nature, and not doctrinal differences as such, are the commonest sources of religious troubles in most communities.

To add another complication to the problem, serious doctrinal discussions are not easily managed when feelings are inflamed by these secondary, but emotionally charged, differences. Many students hold that issues of this type, rather than irreconcilable doctrinal divergence, separate the Orthodox and the Catholics.

If such is the case, then rank-and-file Catholics at the

community level may be able to contribute more than they realize to the work of unity. Already they help with their prayers. But there may be many opportunities for more direct and personal contacts. These can be explored in the chapter to follow.

Roads to Religious Peace

We have noted the differences between high-level doctrinal discussions among the Churches, and community problems of harmony and tolerance. The first are more apt to emphasize the intellectual and the historical. The second may be more personal, a matter of the heart.

How is the neighborhood or the community to promote a pattern of religious harmony? Perhaps the first way to answer this question is to change its wording. We might better say: What can individual Catholics do to promote better understanding and good feeling where religious diversity exists? The reason for the changed wording is important. If any change or reform is needed, it is better to begin at home, and not try to reform the other person first.

If we can visualize a typical community which we can call Middletown, U.S.A., some incidents may arise that cause religious tension. Let us assume that a non-Catholic group was mainly responsible for the incidents. The response may be a blast from Catholic sources. Then everyone rallies to the cause. Persons not involved in the original trouble are now drawn in. The second state of that community is worse than the first.

There was another way of handling the incidents.

Catholic authorities might have had quiet conversations with responsible and friendly elements of the non-Catholic population. They might have asked suggestions for meeting the situation. Calm consideration might lead to any of several methods of action, ranging from ignoring the incidents to a dignified and moderate reply. Thus, instead of uniting the non-Catholic community against us, we would have the best elements on our side, isolating and rebuking their irresponsible members.

The approach of moderation and Christian charity involves many steps. It should begin with the attitudes taught to Catholic children. They must, of course, learn that the Catholic Faith is divinely revealed. They must hold that other faiths are at least incomplete and often in positive error. But such views are not incompatible with respect for the sincerity and faith of non-Catholics. We can even admire their reverence for the Bible and their works of compassion and kindness. God can and does work through those who, through no fault of their own, may not have the fullness of revealed truth.

It is always helpful to seek out qualities that we can admire, rather than those we may deplore. One Protestant minister may work hard in the area of juvenile delinquency. Another may be tireless in visiting the sick. A third may be devoted to the poor. These qualities should be honestly recognized as Christlike works of mercy. Whenever possible, troublemakers and sowers of dissension should be ignored. After all, we have the same troubles within our own Church, witness the Epistles of St. Paul, if no more recent examples come to mind.

When we deal with the non-Catholic world, we con-

99

front a state of mind quite different from our own. Hence there is room for a considerable amount of misunderstanding. It certainly does not help if we quickly take as insults incidents where no harm is really meant. A priest may find it irritating to be addressed as "Mister" or "Reverend," but many people are not aware of proper usage. After all, priests were called "Mister" by one of our first cardinals. And bishops are called "Monsignor" in Rome. Only when an incident is repeated after the error has been explained can we assume that a slight was meant.

As noted above, it is not usually wise to reply in kind to deliberate insults. The psychological reasons for moderation are obvious, as stated before. For religious reasons for moderation, one need only consult the Sermon on the Mount, and countless other passages counseling forgiveness, meekness, and gentleness. Often a probing examination of conscience may reveal that our alleged "zeal for the truth" may also contain elements of wounded feelings, hurt pride, or even plain insecurity.

We should be most sensitive to the danger of confusing certainty in religious faith with inerrancy in personal conduct. The Catholic Church has preserved intact the deposit of divine revelation. But not everything that Catholics do or say is equally right. If the Church itself restricts papal infallibility to rare solemn pronouncements, we may be safe in assuming that the average Catholic does not possess greater powers than the Vicar of Christ.

Hence certainty about the Faith should not lead to personal arrogance in individual judgments about matters not of faith. We know that dishonesty is morally wrong, but we may not be equally certain that a particular practice in the Stock Exchange or in collective bargaining is dishonest. To apply moral principles accurately in such situations, we must have adequate knowledge of the facts and ability to assess and interpret them. "Short selling" on the stock market literally is selling something that one does not have. Yet it is doubtful that an informed moralist, who understood securities speculation, would call short selling dishonest.

Arrogance is a special temptation for us, since we not only have a divinely revealed faith, but also a teaching authority commissioned by God. But the institution of the Church did not abrogate Christ's commands to love one's neighbor and to practice humility. Nothing can help relations with non-Catholics more than admission that we too have been wrong in matters of conduct and judgment. Pope John XXIII has urged this point repeatedly.

It is rather hard to remain angry with someone whose attitude may be summed up in these words: "My faith is of God, and in reverence to him I must profess and defend it; but my failures and mistakes are my own, and these I freely confess."

All these points may be classed as attitudes needed to avoid or lessen religious tension. They should be supplemented by other attitudes that will positively bring about better feelings. Examples were cited earlier about possibilities in the fields of social justice and public morality. In areas such as race relations or protecting youth from pornography, much can be said for a community approach to the problem. Inspiration can be derived from the Faith, but programs of action can be civic. Such programs are fairly common already, but the more they can be extended in suitable areas, the more we can obtain fruitful and harmonious contacts with the non-Catholic community.

Undoubtedly one of the major results of Vatican Council II will be an intensifying of interreligious contacts. Within the Church, the defensive mentality that stemmed from Reformation times is yielding to a more eirenic approach. We speak of "separated brethren," not "heretics." We are more inclined to characterize other faiths as incomplete, rather than erroneous. We recognize the part played by our own failings in the events that ruptured the unity of the Christian Church. All these changes make it much easier for Protestant and Orthodox to see and understand the position of the Catholic Church.

But the crowning work of reconciliation will come from our own personal lives. The effect of prayer, penance, and the example of Christlike living will be decisive. All the other points noted thus far are merely preparatory. This point can hardly be overstressed.

How constant is our prayer for religious unity and the conversion of the Communist world? Is it just a matter of occasional devotions, such as the First Saturdays or the special ceremonies when war threatens? Or is it as constant as we can possibly achieve? For example, we could make it a practice anytime we pass a Protestant Church or Jewish synagogue to repeat our Lord's prayer: "That they may be one, Father." Whenever the radio or television brings up some irritating incident connected with Communism, we could pray: "Father, forgive them, for they know not what they do." Surely we could imitate the Master to this extent.

But the one element that seems really understressed is

that of penance. Pope John XXIII, with his customary gentleness, has several times suggested that the sick and bedridden offer their sufferings and pains for the cause of religious unity and the work of the Ecumenical Council. Surely it is in the spirit of this request to broaden it to all Catholics. We may not be suffering from physical ills, but none of us is free from the constant irritations and trials of life. Instead of letting these be a source of anger, we might quietly offer our mental sufferings as reparation for the world's sins and our offering for the cause of religious unity.

This should be a special concern for those troubled by the warning of Fatima. We might ask ourselves: Have we made as many acts of penance, as requested by our Lady, as we have indulged in denunciations of Communist evils? Could we promise her to match every denunciation of Communism we make with a corresponding act of penance and reparation for their wrongdoings? This could be interior penance, such as quiet acceptance of the trials of life, or it could be exterior penance of a type that would not hurt our health, such as cutting down on smoking or the drinking of alcoholic liquors.

Of course, if we are to do this, it must be done in the spirit of the Gospels. Our Lord says of those who practice ostentatious penance that "they already have had their reward." Acts of penance, of the type described, should be a secret between us and God. More strenuous forms, which are not advised, should be subject to the judgment of a confessor.

If we practice prayer, especially the prayer of forgiveness and quiet prayer frequently repeated during the day, and add to this humble, unostentatious penance, our lives will gradually be changed. In a few months, our family, friends, and associates will notice a difference. This difference will not only bring grace from heaven for the causes mentioned above, but the force of our example will be a direct stimulus to religious peace and, ultimately, to unity.

Religious Tolerance

One of the thorniest issues involving Catholic political teaching is that of religious tolerance. It was discussed widely during the political campaign of 1960. But independently of this particular occasion of controversy, uncertainty about Catholic teaching on religious tolerance is a traditional obstacle to Protestant-Catholic understanding.

The objections in their crudest form feature the Inquisition, current restrictions on Protestant activities in some so-called Catholic countries, and the teaching of certain Catholics that the state has a duty to repress error, including religious error.

We do not effectively answer these objections by listing similar situations prevailing in nations that have a non-Catholic state religion. Those who hold that restrictions upon religious freedom are wrong are not impressed by similar wrongs found in Protestant or Moslem states. Moreover, they say that Catholics repress minority religious groups because of Catholic doctrine. By contrast, they assert, repressive practices in other nations have various historical origins not connected with the doctrine of the state religion. And these questions must be faced.

At any rate, mutual recrimination is rarely fruitful. Pope John XXIII on several occasions suggested that Catholics would help the ecumenical spirit by admitting our own faults instead of publicizing those of others. In this vein, it is well to admit that there is much in our record that gives cause for legitimate concern.

Once this admission is made, we are in a better position to note the special circumstances of history and national temperament that led to the Inquisition and related activities. But even more important, we can face the even tougher problem of Catholic doctrine with respect to religious toleration.

Perhaps the best approach to this, given a serious and thoughtful inquirer, is to recommend a recent *Protestant* study of the problem. In 1959, the World Council of Churches published a brochure entitled "Roman Catholicism and Religious Liberty."* This study should be mandatory reading for any columnist, commentator, or writer who discusses the Catholic position on religious tolerance.

The author, Dr. A. F. Carrillo de Albornoz, summarizes his study in these three points.

"Many Roman Catholic theologians, in many countries, defend a new theory in favor of complete religious liberty in *principle*, . . .

"This theory has in no way been condemned but, on the contrary, is supported by very important members of

---

* It can be obtained in the United States for one dollar from the World Council of Churches, 475 Riverside Drive, New York.

the Roman Catholic Hierarchy; and . . .

"This theory is not a tactical variant of the old doctrine for reasons of opportunism, but another radical and irreducible doctrinal position which is very sincerely and fiercely fighting the old one."

In the introduction to his study, the author notes "the momentous importance, within the Roman Catholic Church, of the every day increasing stream in favor of religious liberty. If such an attitude should prevail in Roman Catholic thinking and practice, there is no doubt that new ways would open toward an ecumenical understanding with our Catholic brethren."

It is amazing, in view of the immense amount of recent writing on Catholic political teaching, that there has been little if any reference to this valuable treatise. In effect, most writers assume that the Catholic Church is basically intolerant. But, if they are friendly to the idea of a Catholic President, they assume that no American Catholic political figure would permit the Church to impose intolerance upon him.

By contrast, this European study concludes that Catholics who uphold the principle of religious liberty, even where the Church may be a state religion, are powerful and probably preponderant in the thinking of the Church. Pope Pius XII, for example, seemed to hold this position in his December, 1953, address to Italian Catholic jurists. He said: "The duty of repressing moral and religious error . . . must be subordinate to *higher and more general* norms, which *in some circumstances* permit, and even perhaps seem to indicate as the better policy toleration of error in order to promote a *greater good.*" He notes

106

that God permits evil. He also cites the parable of the cockle. His predecessor, Pope Pius XI, spoke of the principle of "freedom of consciences" (in *Non Abbiamo Bisogno*).

If this is the view of recent popes, what is the source of the controversy? Basically it stems from several views upheld both in theory and practice by many Catholic theologians. The basic principle is that "error has no rights." Following from this is the conclusion that the State has the duty to repress error, as contrary to the general welfare of a Catholic community. Passages in statements by Popes Gregory XVI, Pius IX, and Leo XIII have been cited to uphold this view as authentic Catholic teaching.

On the other hand, reputable Catholic theologians have also held that, while error has no rights, people who in good faith embrace erroneous views do have the right to freedom of conscience. Some would also state that it is not the function of the State to interfere with private belief, when this does not affect public order. St. Thomas Aquinas taught that it is not the duty of the State to promote all that is good or repress all that is evil or erroneous, but only to deal with matters that affect the common good.

At this stage, many Catholic readers are likely to be puzzled, wondering about the unity of doctrine in the Church. Under the circumstances, we can hardly blame non-Catholics for not understanding, since they have an even stronger view of the unity of Catholic thought. Here is where the distinctions made earlier come into play. The basic principles of revealed doctrine and the natural moral law are unchanging. But it is often most difficult to apply them with accuracy and consistency in complex circumstances of daily life.

An example might make this clear. A person is driving an automobile along a narrow road, with steep ravines on either side. Suddenly a pedestrian looms into sight. The driver could not brake the car in time. To swerve to the left involves a possible head-on collision. To swerve to the right invites possible fatal injury in the ravine. Keeping straight ahead means injury or even death to the pedestrian. What is the moral obligation of the driver?

If the first principle that comes to his mind is that of charity and justice toward the pedestrian, he would risk his own life to avoid a collision. By contrast, if he thinks first of the duty to save his own life, he will try to brake the car but he will not swerve. Both principles are valid. But in this concrete case, they are in conflict.

In the controversy under discussion, at least four points of view can be advocated. The strictest, and most out of harmony with American opinion, is that error has no rights and that the State should repress error. This view may be one of several factors that explain the Inquisition.

A milder view is that expressed by Pope Pius XII, namely, that religious toleration is permissible or even desirable in terms of the general good of a community. He explicitly invokes the higher principle of the common good as taking precedence over any alleged duty of the State to repress error.

A third position would not challenge the theoretical arguments behind the first view, but would maintain that, for tactical reasons, a Catholic State today should not invite the discord that would be involved in suppressing error. This position was often expressed by Catholic writers in the 1928 political campaign here.

The fourth position, that only *persons* have rights, and the one that Dr. Carrillo de Albornoz considers in the ascendancy in the Church today, flatly comes out for freedom of conscience as a sound principle. The state would have neither the right nor the duty to interfere with this freedom, unless the common good so demanded. If, for example, some primitive religion believed in human sacrifice, a state would be obliged to repress this practice. But it might not forbid the worship of idols, however repugnant this might be to the rulers of the state.

Controversies of this nature are not new in the Church. Sometimes they may involve matters of faith not yet clarified by solemn papal definition or a decision by an Ecumenical Council. More often they are in the area of prudential judgment, involving the selection among valid principles (as in the case of the automobile driver cited above). Such controversies do not affect the unity of revealed doctrine.

Once this position is understood, we can allow for a good deal of puzzlement among non-Catholics. It would be amazing if one Catholic layman in a thousand could correctly explain the Syllabus of Errors of Pope Pius IX. This is a summary of errors condemned under his pontificate. It can only be understood by going back to the original decrees of condemnation, and considering them in all their circumstances. When they are quoted out of this historical context, they can indeed be misleading.

This point is well expressed by Dr. Carrillo de Albornoz.

He notes the historical background that explains positions that seem strange and even inconsistent today. We Catholics in the United States, facing the difficult discussions of the coming years, can indeed be grateful for such a book. Indeed, readers might wish to purchase a copy and then recommend it to the next columnist or commentator who assumes that religious intolerance is basic Catholic doctrine.

But religious tolerance does not mean religious indifference. The Catholic Church does try to form the consciences of its members on moral issues in political life. So do Protestant and Jewish circles. Such religious formation does not constitute political dictation over a government official. Failure to understand this distinction is particularly common when religious groups advise their members to support or to oppose particular political parties or candidates. Yet such action may be nothing more than applying religious or moral principles to a concrete civic problem. But church leaders can help avoid misunderstandings by intervening sparingly in political matters, confining their guidance to clear and definite moral or religious problems.

A Catholic as President

In the political climate of 1960, a writer needed a good reason to discuss the idea of a Catholic in the White House. So much had been written on the topic that the average reader was likely to be wearied. Unfortunately most of the public discussions about a Catholic candidate were superficial. They dealt with surface issues that affected only a small segment of the voting public. The issues beneath the surface were far more decisive.

By surface issues are meant the obvious, traditional public attacks upon the Church and Catholic candidates. They were often expressed in crude terms of outright bigotry. Literature of this type was circulated in the states of Wisconsin and Ohio, and appeared in West Virginia. The quantity increased as the campaign continued.

Some of the charges were framed in more scholarly and polite terms. Popes and theologians were quoted on Church-State relations. The Inquisition was exhumed once more. A writer might assert that a Catholic has every right to be President. But, of course, such a candidate had to publicly and regularly proclaim his independence of Church authority, even on doctrinal matters.

From the viewpoint of cold, political analysis, these surface attacks did not seem to be very important. While they stirred up a segment of the population that would never vote for a Catholic for President, they also boomeranged in favor of a Catholic candidate. This type of attack was about the only catalyst that could produce a solid Catholic voting bloc. It was no coincidence that public-opinion polls showed a sharp upswing for President Kennedy *after* a period of stormy public debate on the Church in public life.

We must always remember that we are not alone in deploring religious intolerance. Millions of Protestants and Jews oppose such conduct in principle. Many of them felt the added shame of considering the image of the United States before the world. We who have the military and economic resources for world leadership showed the moral weakness of racial and religious intolerance.

From the point of view of political analysis, the effect of bigotry upon important segments of the non-Catholic population was very important. If some Catholics felt that they were being put on trial because of their religion, there were many Protestants who felt that some of their spokesmen were betraying them. Quite a few nationally prominent clergymen, who were considered the exponents of a vigorous and liberal Christianity, had their reputations at least temporarily tarnished. For in wielding the tar brush, they accumulated more of the tar than they dispensed.

Not to be confused with these were the Protestants, Jews, and secularists who had genuine reservations about the political power of the Catholic Church. Their objection was not to our religious beliefs, but to events in our past or even current history. Another type to consider is the nominal Protestant. Such a person is considered Protestant, but his church-going may be only sporadic. And there are millions in the United States not affiliated to any Church. Finally, there was a group composed of Protestants, Jews, and the unchurched, who reacted against dictation by political parsons.

These factors, added to the geographic distribution of Protestants who opposed in principle a Catholic President, led to startling conclusions. Quite a few persons now hold that, confining the issue of religion to the narrow scope mentioned earlier, Catholicism was an asset, not a liability, to the candidate for the Presidency. Attacks created sympathy for the underdog.

But these surface issues were not decisive in assessing

112

the religious element in politics in 1960. A number of underlying factors must also be considered. They were often intangible; difficult both to state and to rebut. Indeed some of them cannot be rebutted directly, since they are based on the very nature of the Church. Attitudes based on these factors could not be called bigoted. They did not lead to any votes against a Catholic candidate. But they led to a number of puzzled voters sitting out the election.

One of the key difficulties was—and is—the fact that Catholics are a people apart. They are different from the majority of Americans. This shows in a number of ways. Catholics do not eat meat on Friday. Priests and sisters wear distinctive garb. We have parochial schools and religious-oriented colleges. Our bishops speak for us on moral issues without prior consultation of the laity. Most of the time the pastor decides church problems without benefit of lay trustees. We impose restrictions upon mixed marriages.

Examples can be multiplied, but they mostly come down to one central point: Ours is a religion of authority and adherence to traditional faith. The pope and bishops teach; they do not merely exhort and explain. They insist upon the stern moral code revealed by God, no matter how much this may clash with contemporary attitudes. The clash is dramatized in such issues as divorce and birth control, but it may well spring up in entirely different areas.

The entirety of this pattern does make us different. Individual items may be duplicated in the non-Catholic community, especially in creeds that give considerable weight to authority and tradition, such as the Lutheran or Orthodox Jewish faiths. This would be even more true for the Orthodox Churches that broke with Rome in the ninth century. But the average American does not make such fine distinctions. To him the Catholic Church alone is different, and possibly slightly alien.

Since the trend toward conformity is so strong in contemporary America, there is bound to be some uneasiness respecting a group that maintains substantially different traditions. Other Americans are not completely at ease when confronted with the situation. Uncertainty leads to at least a mild form of distrust.

This sense of aloofness is deepened by the fact that many Americans find the Catholic clergy an isolated group. Generally priests shy away from interfaith meetings. They are not available on short notice to participate in radio or television discussions. Nor do they readily sign up for causes of a controversial character. They may not be members of popular clubs or societies in a community. Paradoxically, non-Catholics who do associate with priests generally find them most friendly and approachable.

Clerical isolation, where it does exist, usually stems from either of two factors. One is that most priests are extremely busy with their routine duties. Like most doctors, they simply do not have the time to participate in a wide range of community activities. What is more, they feel inhibited by the very fact that they are considered to speak for the Church. They would not accept certain assignments without prior permission of their bishop. Consequently they very often turn down invitations that

114

other clergy might accept on the basis of a telephone call.

There is very little of a substantive nature that we can do to change this picture. So much of it is tied closely to doctrinal orthodoxy and the God-given character of the Church that it is bound to remain a characteristic of Catholics in our society. Some individual Catholics make concessions as they feel the pressure for conformity. But if essentials are involved, they cannot yield without compromising the integrity of their faith.

Other areas of difference are more tactical than doctrinal. Many non-Catholics are still disquieted by fears or even convictions that Catholics may form an unwholesome power bloc. They cite a number of instances in which we have tried to influence public policy or morals. Campaigns for decency in motion pictures and in print, efforts to secure bus rides on public buses for parochial school children, and views on legislation involving divorce or birth control are often interpreted as dangerous abuses of power.

Many who would ignore charges that the Vatican is trying to control American life are deeply concerned over alleged pressure tactics by American Catholics. The objectors are not worried over the source of these actions— i.e., whether they are dictated by the hierarchy or simply the work of lay Catholics in a local area—they object to the use of political power to secure the objectives of any religious group.

Some of these objections could be overcome if we were more willing to approach problems of public morality on a community basis. On such matters there should be no objection to a formula such as this: Motivation from the

Church; action in harmony with all citizens concerned over public morals. To be specific, while the Legion of Decency performs a very useful function for Catholics nationally, it may not be wise for Catholics unilaterally to try to persuade theater owners to follow its listings. When we condemn a picture as immoral, it should not be too difficult to persuade parents of other faiths to try to keep such fare from family theaters. Even more effective is the effort to emphasize the positive and to create a market for wholesome films.

It will be more difficult to meet the problems inherent in the feeling that Catholics are different and noncon-formist. But we can do much about this. Indeed, the Catholic concern for Christian unity should be a far more powerful reason for attempting to bridge the gulf of isolation.

We cannot do this, of course, by any compromise in doctrine and practice. We would not even gain respect by passing over differences in silence. But we can do a great deal if all of us became much better Catholics than we are. As was noted in the opening chapter of this book, a Catholic who is kind, humble, prayerful, and compas-sionate is the best argument for the truth of our faith. In such cases, outsiders not only note a difference, but also they see that this difference is most attractive.

Thus, the spotlight focused upon the Church today can be turned into a blessing, instead of a source of irritation and resentment. In general, let us ignore the extremists and bigots. But to others who do not understand us, let us extend the open hand of kindly friendship. This will gain us respect and understanding. It will give Catholics a status in the United States that they could never win by angry retort or pitting power against power. A fullness of the Catholic spirit will certainly enshrine the Church in the hearts of millions that do not understand it today. And this result is infinitely more important than the prestige of having a Catholic President.

Never since the days of the Reformation have we had such opportunities as exist today to approach our separated brethren in a spirit of understanding and kindly interest. They are seeking to know us better and to work with us in many areas of common concern. Any pettiness or selfishness on our part could raise obstacles to the work of reunion, so magnificently begun by Pope John XXIII. "So let your light shine before men, in order that they may see your good works and give glory to your Father in heaven" (Mt 5:16).

VI

The Catholic Image in Political Life

The Catholic and Politics

We are told in the Gospels not to bury our talents. The Word of God and the truths of faith are not merely the private property of believers. They are to influence society so that men will find it easier to live in accord with God's laws.

In discussing problems of modern society, and their implications for the apostolic Catholic, the emphasis thus far has been upon social problems of the local community. But the community is not an isolated unit. For better or worse, it is influenced by broad political and economic trends, on both a national and an international scale. Any inquiry into the mission of the Catholic in the world, if it is to be complete, must include these elements.

When the subject of the Catholic and politics is raised, our minds normally turn to concrete issues. We think of current controversies, such as the legality of Catholic children's riding in buses provided by community funds. Or we may think of even more direct impacts of the political process. Examples here would be taxes, community improvements that may benefit our neighborhood, or political leaders who may be in a position to extend favors to us.

Thus politics is often cast in the mold of self-interest—

118

that is, how much we must give as compared with how much we may receive. Personal attitudes of this nature tend to color the whole process of government with a taint of self-interest. If constituents want to give as little as possible and receive as much as possible, it would be remarkable if political leaders did not adopt the same thinking. The result is a deterioration of politics in the public mind. As a profession it is often considered somewhat less than honorable.

These attitudes may seem surprising in the light of American history and the political teaching of Catholic writers of all ages. In the early years of our country, the holding of public office was a great privilege. Outstanding representatives of the nation felt honored to be elected to a post of power and responsibility. Partly because we had such high caliber of representatives in Colonial assemblies, we were able to find sterling leaders in the great crises that led to the War of Independence. These able men, after early failure, worked out a Constitution that is almost unique in the history of the world.

Even today, after a long deterioration in political life, which produced notorious scandals in the last century and in the present, the American people still have a strong residue of respect for the political process. Side by side with our cynicism about politicians is a feeling that a high office, of itself, commands respect. We are not really happy when our worst fears are translated into reality. Our nation is at its vigorous best when it has strong and intelligent leadership.

While the public may downgrade politics as a profession, able men still are impelled to seek office. This is especially true in times of crisis, when thousands make heavy financial sacrifices to serve their country. The vote of confidence of an electorate, and the opportunity of service, are often enough to overcome the personal attacks that discourage less hardy souls.

Catholic reaction to government and political life has changed somewhat through the centuries. The New Testament did not go extensively into the problem. Our Lord told Pilate that whatever power he had, he had from above. The Lord also paid taxes. St. Paul told the early Christians to obey civil authorities as speaking with the power of God. St. Peter had a similar message. While these first Catholics agreed that civil authority was of God, they disagreed on other phases of the question.

St. Augustine, for example, felt that political subjection was a result of original sin. St. Thomas, in a view now generally accepted, held that political life was natural to man, a direct result of his social nature. It was not a punishment for sin. Other early controversies concerned the relationship of the civil state to the Church. Catholic thinking evolved to the point where both societies were considered sovereign in their own spheres. But there is still debate about situations where their jurisdictions overlap, as, for example, in marriage and divorce.

The Church has consistently held that the *form* of government is, of itself, no concern of religion. Provided only that the rule is just, it is not important that the type of government be a democracy, an aristocracy, or single-man rule. Many secular writers think that the Church is prejudiced against democracy. The origin of this view is twofold: first, the writings of Pope Leo XIII, in a context of

120

violent anticlericalism and anti-Catholic "liberalism" in newly formed democracies of Western Europe, sounded notes of caution about abuses in democracy; and secondly, in the present century, many of the world's dictatorships have sprung up in Catholic (or nominally Catholic) nations.

Yet persons with a longer view of history would have been less hasty to reach such conclusions. The Church has long held in high regard the idea of rule by law, rather than by the whim of ruler. Even under medieval serfdom, the prevailing judgment was that any lord or baron must rule under law. The insistence upon this point was the basis of the Magna Carta. It was also the ground for the revolt of Catholic writers against the concept of the divine rule of kings. And law, in the Middle Ages, had a strong element of insistence upon the consent of the governed.

Pope Pius XII made two major contributions to Catholic theory of government. His Christmas, 1944, message was a long tribute to democracy. While reaffirming traditional neutrality as to the form of government, he raised the question whether, in modern times, the democratic form of rule might not be a virtual necessity. Given the immense power of the modern state over its citizens, would it be possible, he asked, to have just rule without participation by the ruled?

Again, in 1953, the Pope made an important address on religious toleration in a modern political community. Many Catholics had opposed toleration of error on the grounds that truth has higher rights that should be upheld. But the Holy Father noted that often the general

121

welfare of the community calls for toleration of lesser evils, for fear that greater goods may be lost in the process of repression.

The points raised thus far may strike many readers as being up in the air, far removed from the tension and excitement of a political campaign—even a contest for the local mayoralty. Yet sound policy and sound practice, in the long run, must be based on the bedrock of accurate theory. When people have a false notion of the nature of man, particularly in relation to government, many dangerous results can follow. One of the basic evils of the Nazi and Communist forms of government has been the subordination of the individual to the state, with the consequent loss of essential rights of the human person. On the other hand, when the power of the state is weakened excessively, as in France before De Gaulle, anarchy can result.

Another point that may strike readers as strange is the fact that there are debates, differences of opinion, and shifts of emphasis in the realm of Catholic political teaching. Some may think that if it is Catholic, then it should be certain and unchanging. Here some distinctions must be made that are most important for the understanding of Catholic political and economic thought.

The first point to note is that very little can be found in the Scriptures or in the Church's solemn doctrinal pronouncements which pertains *directly* to the political and economic field. We noted some passages indicating that civil authority is from God. The Church has solemnly condemned Communism and Socialism, as defined at the time of papal condemnation. But the bulk of Catholic political and economic teaching is based on natural law. Natural law is known, in this context, from the study of human nature and society, in the light of right reason. It may take centuries for theologians to agree upon, and the Church to affirm, truths of this nature.

Secondly, many points in the Church's political and economic teaching are derived as conclusions or applications of revealed teaching or of natural law. Such doctrines as the law of love of neighbor or membership in the Mystical Body of Christ may seem quite remote from technical problems of industrial relations. Yet, after profound thinking on their implications, we may see that the logical consequence of these truths is a pattern of conduct that affects the factory or the mine.

When we assert the dignity of the human person, as having a soul created by Almighty God, we do not directly say anything about race relations or wages paid to heads of families. Yet it could well be that race relations and wages may involve practices that are incompatible with our proper relations with a fellow child of God. It is for this reason that the Church, especially in recent years, has often spoken on such issues. When glaring evils make it clear that society is not functioning properly, it is only proper that the moral implications of these evils be made clear.

If all these distinctions are complex, and even confusing, it is to the good. For they should keep us from the dangerous habit of rushing into complex situations with a simple remedy, offered in the name of the Church. Some issues are that simple. But many more in the modern world are not. Moderation, caution, and careful study are not signs of compromise. Often they indicate the only course that a wise and humble Catholic should take.

Political Attitudes of Catholics

There are two reasons why it may be difficult to think as a Catholic in political matters. The first was hinted at earlier, when we noted the complexity and even the changing character of Catholic political teaching. We shall develop this point somewhat farther and then go into the second difficulty. This latter is nothing more than the usual problem of applying general principles to the infinitely complex issues of everyday life.

Many Catholics are astonished when we speak of the political or social teaching of the Church. Their instinctive reaction is to ask: What has this to do with religion? The answer is clear. Religion in the narrow sense of faith and worship can be divorced from political and social life. But conditions prevailing in the world deeply affect the organized practice of religion. Communist Russia and Nazi Germany furnish good illustrations of this truth. In such cases the Church cannot remain indifferent to conditions that vitally affect her children.

But there is another function of revealed religion. In addition to faith and worship of God, religion involves codes of conduct based on God's law. This law may be revealed directly by God, or it may be known only by human reason. In either case, the Church as the supreme guardian of the moral law has both the right and the duty to preach it in its fullest implications.

The moral law covers the entirety of man's life: his

124

working life, his political life, his family life. This does not mean that every decision we make necessarily involves moral judgment. Some decisions are purely technical, such as weighing the value of one automobile as compared with another when we are in the market for a new family car. But the way we drive an automobile, since it affects the safety and lives of others, has important moral implications.

Political life is partly technical, partly moral. An example of the technical would be the method of ruling. In the United States we have separation of powers between the executive and the legislature. In England, the executive power is selected by the leading party in Parliament. These are techniques of ruling, and it is rare that they would involve any clear-cut moral issue.

On the other hand, there are political actions that definitely involve morality. It is certainly unjust to jail opposition leaders on the sole grounds that they belong to the political opposition. Grafting is dishonest. So is stealing elections.

Between these extremes of the strictly technical and the obviously moral is the complex, in-between ground that can be the subject of much controversy. For example, there is the obligation to vote. Voting in the Indian State of Kerala is a serious obligation for any Catholic. Failure to vote would mean the re-election of a Communist legislature. But in a dictatorship that stages "show" elections, failure to vote or the casting of blank ballots may be the only form of protest. Two opposite modes of action may be proper in different circumstances.

We note the complexity faced in applying moral law

to political life for two reasons. First, this explains the somewhat hesitant and even apparently contradictory nature of Church teaching on political matters. Nineteenth-century popes were warning the faithful about abuses in the democratic process. They had sound historical reasons for doing so. Twentieth-century popes, against a different historical background, are far more worried about dictatorship and excessive concentration of political power.

Secondly, since the application of moral principles in this concrete area is so difficult, we should be most tolerant toward our fellow Catholics who may disagree with us on such applications. This can be seen when we apply principles to one of the most controversial areas of American politics, the question of school desegregation.

The Catholic bishops of the United States have spoken clearly and unequivocally on the morality of racial discrimination. They condemned it as un-Christian. They further offer as their considered judgment the conclusion that segregation of itself involves such discrimination. Logically, this applies to school segregation.

Does this judgment close the issue for Catholics? It does, so far as principle is concerned. But the application of this principle in the political process involves a number of concrete choices, among which good Catholics might differ. Should integration be immediate and total, or gradual and selective? Would it be better to start with the early grades, because children lack prejudice; or at the high-school level, because they can be reasoned with and given sound arguments?

Some Catholics might argue that the ultimate goal of

racial harmony would better be served by a slow process of education and piecemeal integration. Others might counter that this only prolongs the argument and will intensify bitterness in the long run. These are prudential judgments, in which men of good faith, seeking the same goal, may differ.

The key words here are "good faith, seeking the same goal." Some persons who advocate a slow approach admittedly are seeking to evade and nullify the decision of the Supreme Court. But others sincerely feel that when an injustice has deep roots in history, change has to be piecemeal and gradual. The essential attitude is willingness to see injustice and to seek effective means to remedy it.

Because of the complexity of political life, American Catholics are found on almost any band of the political spectrum. Some may be identified with the liberal views commonly associated with the Americans for Democratic Action. Others may prefer to take their politics from the *National Review*. Many are independent of both wings. We may disagree with the judgment of those with whom we differ. But it would be rash and un-Christian to question their loyalty, either to Church or country.

This does not mean that our faith should not affect our political thinking. On the contrary, it should. But we would deceive ourselves if we were to believe that, because we try to think and vote in accord with God's law, this will be an easy process. On the contrary, it will call for painstaking study and appraisal of both men and issues.

The fact that our intentions are right and our goals are sound is no guarantee that we are espousing the best means for achieving these goals. Nearly everyone in the United States sincerely seeks peace. We all oppose Communism. But these aims and intentions do not automatically give us the answer to concrete questions currently debated in the United States.

Will a series of summit meetings promote an honorable peace? Are they more likely to lead to Communist gains? Are cultural exchanges with Iron Curtain countries a trap? Or are they opening wedges that may lead to more freedom in such nations and the eventual destruction of Communism? Are loyalty oaths for college students seeking Federal loans wise and useful?

Far too many of us answer such questions by a quick and emotional assertion: I favor peace and I abhor Communism and consequently I favor/oppose summit meetings, cultural exchange, and student loyalty oaths. This type of answer confuses goals with certain debatable steps toward these goals.

These points are spelled out at some length, because this process of thinking has often caused the most grievous types of division within the Catholic fold. The great Cardinal Newman was denounced to Rome as suspect of heresy because he allegedly was not worried about Italian seizure of the Papal States. There were French Catholics sixty years ago who suspected the faith of their compatriots who supported the Republic and did not want a return of the monarchy.

Perhaps it is well for all of us to remember that teaching authority in the Church belongs only to the pope and the bishops. Infallible decisions are confined to certain solemn pronouncements of popes and Ecumenical Councils. Apart from these cases, all of us are prone to error, even when acting in good faith and applying sound principles. The devil in the case is the complexity of concrete issues in any given historical setting.

None of this implies that we should be timid or irresolute in trying to make God's law a vital force in everyday life. But we should always be prepared to distinguish between eternal truth and our own application of it at any time. If our position is the result of careful study and thought, by all means let us defend it on its merits. But let us defend it humbly, crediting the good faith of opponents until the contrary is proved beyond doubt.

Our faith is not an electronic machine that instantaneously gives answers to the most complex questions. What it does give us is a set of moral principles about political society. It impels us to seek the common good of our country and of the world. It makes us advocates of peace, justice, integrity, honor. It encourages us to see every man as our brother under God. But it does not absolve us from the hard and tedious task of prudence and political wisdom, as we seek to make principles living realities.

Practical Problems of Politics

Should the fact that we are Catholics make any difference in our political thinking? This is not as simple a question as it might seem. Obviously any firmly held religious belief should make a difference in practical life. But are Catholics, practicing their faith, substantially at odds with others who may be Orthodox, Protestant, or Jewish?

129

Experience seems to indicate that, on most issues, they will think and act alike. Catholic leaders of France, Germany, and Italy are not at odds with Protestant leaders of Great Britain and the United States. Catholics show no special voting pattern in Congress. There have been excellent Catholic governors and mayors, and there have been poor ones. Some notorious political machines have been largely Catholic, but others equally bad have not.

In practice, the more important distinction seems to be personal integrity and practice of faith, not theological differences. This is but another way of stating what we said before: Catholic political theory is based more on natural law than on revealed doctrine. We might apply this distinction to some practical problems of politics.

The average citizen has several contacts with the political process. He votes. He may be active in a political party. He may seek to influence officials of government. He pays taxes and obeys laws.

Much has been written on the obligation to vote. It is considered a civic duty. Many writers consider it a moral obligation as well. This is clear when some great issue is at stake, such as preventing the election of a Communist government. But apart from such clear-cut cases, the common good of the community and our concern for our fellow man should make us interested in government. And the interested citizen votes.

It would be enlightening to know how many examine their consciences on *how* they vote? Do we think before we vote? Are we blind followers of one party or one political leader? Are we concerned with the good of the whole community, or merely with our selfish interests?

How many of us have the standard: "Everybody is getting government money. Why not me?"

In principle, we have little respect for those who have a double standard of conduct, one for the public eye and another for private practice. Yet many who would condemn gross selfishness in their ordinary dealings make exceptions for political life (or even for driving an automobile). Here is where integrity, total practice of one's faith, is important.

Is voting for a candidate because he is Catholic, or Italian, or Irish, or a fellow club-member wrong? It certainly would be wrong if this meant picking an inferior candidate. Considerations of religion or national background should not in themselves be decisive. There may be times when circumstances should change this rule. Other things being equal, I would vote for a qualified Negro as an effort to break down racial prejudice.

But the Catholic who really wants to promote honest and efficient government does not wait until the general election to do his duty. The general election offers a choice among candidates nominated by political parties. But the really important decisions are those affecting the nominations. If both parties pick low-grade candidates, what choice does one have at general elections?

Interest in nominations does not mean merely voting in primary elections. Again, this is a late stage in the electoral process. Primary elections choose among those who seek office. Hence the real problem is to get able candidates interested in public life.

This interest has to be practical. Normally one cannot present himself to a party leader at the last minute and say, "I am ready to run for mayor." Few politicians, and few corporation presidents, start at the top. The first steps involve years of working with political machines and accepting minor offices.

A proper interest in political life does not mean that every eligible Catholic has to be in politics. Rather it means that each should do his part, according to his abilities and opportunities. We might show our civic interests by taking part in meetings, drives, committees. We can encourage those who join political clubs or seek office. And above all, we should avoid the negative and corrosive attitude of cynicism. We do not automatically attribute unworthy motives to those who are in politics.

Our faith should affect our attitude toward government officials, whether elected or appointed. One point frequently overlooked is that such persons should be shown kindness and courtesy. It is a good idea to commend them for services done, especially for efficiency and enthusiasm in their work. People commonly write or phone to complain. A Christian should be at least equally willing to express gratitude, both to the official concerned and to his superiors.

A person of integrity should abhor graft and the seeking of special favors. Nearly everyone condemns the official who takes bribes. But, in the United States, it is quite rare that an official demands a bribe to do his duty. Corruption almost always means that an official is asked to violate or evade the law. Is it too much to say that the person who solicits such "favors" is more guilty than the corrupt public servant?

Nor should we excuse the seeking of special privilege on

132

the ground that the matter involved is minor. Obviously the "fixing" of a parking ticket is no great crime. It might not be wrong at all, if the adjustment is based on sound grounds. No one would condemn a doctor on an emergency call for parking in a loading zone, instead of wasting precious minutes looking for an empty space for his car.

But when a person is clearly and inexcusably guilty of a violation, he lessens respect for law by seeking a ticket adjustment. If the traffic violation is more serious—for example, speeding—then it is even worse to evade punishment. There should be no privileged class that feels entitled to drive dangerously.

By contrast, there may be times when one can and even should conscientiously intercede for a wrongdoer. It often happens that a solid citizen is arrested for some crime committed years back when he was wild and unruly. If he has lived down this past, it certainly seems that the interests of justice would be served by either a dismissal of the indictment or a suspended sentence. Clemency of this type is usually possible without any infringement of law or community customs.

Finally, in this context, theft from government is still theft. Persons who would return ten cents wrongly taken from individuals seem blind when government or corporations are involved. They may seek to use city workmen and materials on private property. Or they may overcharge on contracts in collusion with dishonest officials. This type of theft is no different from stealing from one's next door neighbor.

We should be sensitive on the matter of paying taxes.

It is true that one can find writers who argue that tax laws do not bind in conscience. But this type of reasoning dates largely from past centuries, when democratic government was not common. In those days taxes were impositions of the sovereign, all too often used for his luxuries or his private wars. Understandably citizens sought to avoid such imposts.

But the modern democratic state has enormous expenses connected with its function of promoting the common good. The United States, for example, currently spends over fifty billion dollars for defense. If we do not like the way the government is spending money, we can use the democratic process to change the policy. We can hardly allow the individual citizen, in a functioning democracy, to decide for himself whether or not he will share the common burden.

Many of the readers of this chapter have very little choice about paying taxes. Income tax is withheld and sales taxes and excises are extracted at every purchase. But others can risk concealing income. It is hardly fair that some few can live quite well, with a minimum of taxes, while others who have heavier personal obligations also have heavier taxes. "Bear ye one another's burdens."

What was said of tax laws should apply to all law. If a particular law seems unwise or even unjust, the remedy is to seek to change the law, not to defy or evade it. Here we refer to the deliberate violation of a serious law. There is such a thing as following the spirit of the law, even though one technically violates the letter. One may cut through formalities and red tape, provided that the purpose of the law is preserved. A driver rushing a critically ill patient to a hospital might only pause at a red light and drive through if no traffic is in sight.

Many of these points seem minor in themselves. But collectively they determine the public attitude toward government and law. We can see a dramatic example of the effect of attitudes in teen-age drivers. When they learn driving from professional teachers, they are not only technically more skillful, but they are far less reckless. When they learn from parents, they are often poorly trained and, what is worse, prone to dangerous and illegal driving.

The important difference here lies in attitudes. If the parent generally exceeds speed limits, eases past stop signs, or even "runs" red lights, his children will do what he does, not what he says. And, being young, they will show much less judgment. Their father may be highly selective in violating traffic ordinances, and may actually be a safe driver.

In the same way, our minor violations of law or corruption of officials may be not too significant, taken individually. But they create a climate that breeds major corruption and serious crime. Integrity should be absolute. Once we compromise on the principle of honesty, and rule of law, we cannot say where the process of corruption will stop.

What Should Government Do?

During election years we hear a great deal about the duties and powers of government. There is debate about the proper course of action in dozens of spheres. There are charges of socialism and the welfare state, and countercharges that vital needs of the people have been neglected. It is no secret that the Republicans play down the function of the federal government. By contrast, Democrats tend to enlarge the scope of its activity.

Is this great debate purely political? Or are there moral issues also involved? Those familiar with the social encyclicals of recent popes should have no difficulty in answering these questions. One of the key subjects that has preoccupied popes, when writing on social problems in the last seventy years, is the proper position of government.

This does not mean that the Church tells us, even by implication, how to choose between the two major political parties in the United States. Even if we were to try to match papal writings against political platforms, we would face a difficult task. Of course, we could be dishonest and pull statements out of historical context. By such methods partisans on either side could find ammunition.

But the serious student of Catholic political teaching will not indulge in such doubtful tactics. He realizes that papal moral teaching is not formulated in a vacuum. Principles do not change, but emphasis and application can differ widely because of changed circumstances.

For example, when Pope Leo XIII wrote "On the Condition of Workers" nearly seventy years ago, he was confronted with some of the worst effects of the industrial revolution. He felt that in many nations government was watching with indifference while workers were being ruthlessly exploited. In consequence, he stressed the need

136

for social legislation and the duty of the state to protect and help the poor.

By contrast, when Pope Pius XII gave his renowned radio addresses and peace messages, the pendulum had swung to the other extreme. Two forms of statism were disturbing the peace of the world: Nazism and Fascism on one side, and Communism on the other. In many nations some form of the welfare state had replaced the indifferent type of nineteenth-century government.

Obviously in this context there would be a considerable difference in emphasis between the two popes. In 1891, governments as a rule did not sufficiently control the abuses that flourished in economic life. In the 1940's and 1950's, quite a few nations went much too far in the opposite direction. Understandably the reaction from the Vatican was different.

We repeat that this does not mean any shift in principle. A wise parent does not use the same techniques with a timid child and one that is outgoing and even boisterous. The basic approach of loving control is the same. But in the one case encouragement is needed, and in the other restraint is the proper approach. The nineteenth-century state was timid in the social sphere. By the middle of the twentieth century, we were plagued with the totalitarian state.

In terms of Catholic political teaching, two fundamental principles are involved. One is the inherent duty of government to seek the common good of its citizens. The other is the obligation to assert the minimum of power needed to fulfil its functions. Sound political leaders will keep both these aims in mind. When either one or the other is neglected, a nation is undoubtedly being misruled.

Another way of stating these guides of conduct is to note that the State should be the servant, not the master, of its citizens. Its main purpose is to maintain orderly conditions, so that individuals and families prosper in peace. It errs in one direction when it permits one group of citizens to exploit and mistreat another. And it errs in the opposite direction when it interferes with basic human rights of its citizens.

A glance at nineteenth-century history shows the abuses tolerated by socially weak governments. Children went to work in factories in their earliest years. At times youngsters of six or seven worked long hours in spinning mills. Women toiled in mines. Men labored twelve or more hours a day, often seven days a week. When panics, caused by greedy speculation, prevailed, the millions out of work were often left to starve. There was no workmen's compensation for injured workers. When banks failed (and they often did) depositors lost their savings.

When all these things were happening, many persons justified the situation as inevitable. They argued that this was the nature of industrial production. Any effort to change it by government action would make conditions worse.

Such arguments were decisively rejected by Popes Leo XIII and Pius XI. They insisted that the welfare of citizens was the first concern of government. They could not accept the contrasts between extreme wealth and bitter poverty as willed by God. On the contrary, the bounty of the earth was created for all. It is the duty of government to provide, by wise rules and laws, for a more fair

138

distribution of this bounty among the whole population.

In this connection, all the recent popes have upheld the principle of union organization and social legislation. They have spoken out on unemployment, housing conditions, the special needs of women and children, and many other related topics. In particular they sought a living wage for families, so that the wage-earner could provide the basic needs in terms of housing, food, clothing, medical care, and savings for emergencies.

Yet, in seeking these goals, we must be careful not to use methods that would make the situation only worse. Pope Leo XIII denounced Socialism and the class struggle as replacing one set of evils by another. The same warnings were repeated by Pope Pius XI. Indeed, his condemnation of Communism in 1937 is a masterpiece that seems to defy the passing of time.

The late Pope Pius XII was even more emphatic in warning against undue concentration of power. After World War II, he tried and often succeeded in alerting the people of Europe to the dangers involved in nationalizing industry. He warned against carrying social legislation to the point that freedom was jeopardized. He feared excessive concentration of power in certain labor unions. He cautioned German Catholics on unsound arguments for giving labor the right to share management powers in industry.

By contrast, Pope John XXIII, seeing the situation in a different perspective, offered a viewpoint often strikingly different from that of his predecessor. In "Christianity and Social Progress" (*Mater et Magistra*) he judged that many social controls in contemporary society could be compatible with sound moral principles. Far from expressing a fear of labor's power, he called for participation of workers in social controls at all levels, from the individual factory to national and international economic councils. Thus changing economic and political conditions can lead to varied concrete and practical recommendations, all based on the same unchanging underlying moral principles.

How does all this affect the thinking of Catholics sensitive to the social teachings of the Church? What is its bearing on issues currently debated, such as medical care for the aged or relief for depressed areas?

These questions can best be answered by stages. First we must ascertain if the problem is really governmental. We must ask if the general welfare is involved. Can the needs be met by private efforts? If government must act, need this action be Federal? It is better to keep power close to the people, and this is more easily achieved when government action is state or local.

It would be ideal, but perhaps politically impossible, to ask that proposals for action be preceded by a competent and impartial study of the needs. In the case of medical care for the aged, we would want facts about the number of older persons who face impossible medical burdens. It would also be helpful to know if the problem could be met by nongovernmental means, such as private insurance, hospitalization plans, and medical programs secured through collective bargaining.

Perhaps in such a study some basic policy problems about American customs of living will arise. Has inflation caused this problem by eroding savings? Or is it mainly

140

a result of our high-consumption economy and its impact on the habit of saving? Have we reached a state in which forced saving—and social security is only forced saving— is necessary for the great mass of our citizens?

It could be that the answers to these questions would favor both Federal action to provide medical care for the aged, and the making of such care a permanent part of our social security system. We might conclude that, in our present culture, most families will not or even can not save enough to meet their medical needs in later years.

These are matters of fact and prudential judgment that cannot be handled by easy generalizations. It is tempting to say that earlier generations managed to get by without government aid. But a few decades ago we did not have such a large percentage of persons living past their productive years. Modern medicine prolongs lives dramatically. Nor was the housing situation the same fifty years ago. Apartment living has made it much more difficult for children to take care of aged parents.

These observations are made to illustrate the difficulty of applying principles, not to prejudge the issue under discussion. We can hope that political discussions will enlighten voters on the extent of the need for government assistance, and the wisdom of the differing proposals to meet this need.

In such issues, the political teachings of the popes offer only broad guidelines that will be interpreted and emphasized differently by individual Catholics. The Church clearly condemns the extremes of indifference to human need and the totalitarian state. It is concerned about human misery, but also about excessive concentration of power in the hands of individuals or even groups.

Within these limits there is ample room for Catholics to be either Democrats or Republicans. We do not have the extremes of social philosophy that exist in certain European nations. Our major parties differ more in emphasis upon means than in terms of ultimate goals. The differences are real and important. But it is unthinkable that Church authorities in the United States would be confronted with the problem that recently faced the Italian bishops. The Italian bishops were forced to warn the faithful against Marxist political parties. By contrast, the political power of Communists and Socialists here is zero. For this we can be thankful.

States' Rights and Federal Power

Catholic political writers, as we have noted, distrust centralization of power, whether this be economic or political. As control becomes physically removed from the citizen, there is the danger that authority may become impersonal or even autocratic. Corruption and waste may be harder to detect and correct. Inefficiency may set in because of sheer multiplication of responsibilities.

Because of this, we hold it wrong for a higher authority to take over duties that can and will be performed adequately by lesser groups. The Federal government should not seek responsibility in areas where state authority is sufficient. Nor should states take over the work of counties or cities. Public officials should not step in when private organizations are doing a needed job.

It is probable that most Americans would agree with

this principle. The difficulty comes in practice, and especially with the concept that the smaller group should be *able and willing* to carry out its responsibilities. The extent of this difficulty can be measured by the enormous growth of the Federal government in the past half-century. Leaving aside the problem of defense, there are nonmilitary departments today that singly spend more than the entire Federal budget of thirty years ago.

This fact has been deplored by public speakers with commendable frequency. Yet little has been done to reverse the trend. Indeed, each new Congress seems to bring forth some new extension of Federal power. A well known book claims that our affluent society is wasting money on luxuries and ignoring public needs—this at a time when the total tax bill is over thirty-two per cent of national income!

The basic assumption behind such arguments is that everything that is in the national interest is a concern of the Federal government. We need more schools, highways, slum clearance, medical education, scientific training, aid to commuter railroads, and sewage disposal plants. It is true that the nation would profit from more of these things. But if the nation wants them, the states, cities, and private groups can provide them.

Two factors help explain this pressure for nationalizing our social responsibilities. One is the desire to get back the tax dollars we pay to the Federal treasury. We know that billions go out in various forms of grants and subsidies. So we want our share. What we fail to realize is that new demands will call for new taxes, and we will be no better than before. Indeed, we may be worse off, since many citizens take a wasteful and irresponsible attitude toward federal money. They may be very careful in spending local funds for schools, but they make extravagant demands upon a federally financed highway system. The fallacy of "free" money leads to weird results.

Another reason for adding responsibility to the Federal government is that for pressure groups success is a one-shot operation. If an organization seeking urban renewal can secure Federal subsidies, then it becomes easy to persuade cities to fight blight and rot. The same program on an exclusively local level might call for several hundred separate campaigns to persuade individual cities to act. At the least, fifty states would need to be convinced that their cities should be saved.

The same is true of the national highway program. Much can be said for a co-ordinated and integrated system of national highways. It would be difficult, but probably not impossible, to secure this by interstate compacts. Possibly some Federal subsidies would still be needed for roads used primarily by through traffic. On the other hand, toll roads might be adequate to meet this need.

Some persons may feel that a job will be done better if it is under Federal control. Presumably our national legislature attracts more competent persons than do state legislatures and city councils. Possibly our Federal departments can hire higher quality administrators than could be secured under state and local salary levels. It seems to be so easy and direct to solve the problem once and for all in Washington.

Another difficulty is the fact that, in spite of contrary theory, citizens may well have more direct control over the national government than they exercise over state and local governments. It is a fact that the quality of some state legislatures is notoriously low. Probably there is more proportionate corruption and inefficiency in many city governments than in our national government. Citizens often overlook local faults, while sternly condemning any frailties unearthed in Washington.

Voters often turn to Washington because state legislatures are not truly representative. In most states of the Union, the cities and suburbs are not given a fair share of legislators. Often the disparity is extreme. This evil is being corrected as a result of Supreme Court intervention. But it has left its impact on our national government, as cities seek federal aid for projects slighted or denied by rural majorities in state legislatures.

Finally, we note that local lack of initiative may not always be due to lack of interest, but only to lack of funds. The total tax burden today is so great that many communities, and even some states, cannot realistically raise funds needed for schools, sewage disposal plants, or urban renewal.

All these points explain, but do not necessarily justify, proposals for ever-increasing Federal powers and expenditures. To complicate the matter, not every advocate of states' rights and local initiative is really calling for state or local action. Often they really want state or local *inaction.* Certainly this seems to be the case when interracial justice is concerned.

It will not be an easy task for the most dedicated advocates of decentralized power to correct the present situation. But certain steps can and should be taken, both by

145

private citizens and by officials of state and local governments.

First, we should agree that private initiative should be favored over government action, unless some clear public harm is threatened.

Second, we should use the level of government closest to the community for all public functions it can handle.

Third, we should experiment widely with co-operative intergovernmental arrangements for problems that cross political boundaries. Such devices as metropolitan authorities and interstate compacts have not been used sufficiently.

Fourth, we should reserve to the Federal government only those responsibilities that are truly national, or exceptionally such public needs that cannot be fully met by state and local authorities.

These principles will be meaningless, however, until the citizen voter is willing to support them in terms of effective political action. It is not sufficient to denounce the Federal government for intruding into such areas as schooling, highway construction, or urban renewal. We must be prepared to take adequate steps to see that real needs are met by local action after the Federal government withdraws.

Unless we do this, we may be demanding an impossible level of heroism from candidates for Federal office. If the voters are concerned only with their needs or desires, and not with the level of government that meets these needs, how many candidates for public office are going to tell them to go to their state legislatures or city councils? Possibly some candidates may risk defeat for high principles in the effort to educate the public. Generally, however, political parties are practical and give the public what it wants.

Ultimately, then, the responsibility lies with the citizen voter. Probably the first realistic step is to educate the voters themselves. They must learn that nothing the government gives is really free. If they want a government service, it is likely to be cheaper, better adapted to their needs, and better administered if it is run by a *responsible* local government.

This in turn demands effective interest in the quality of local and state governments. Interest calls for continual participation in the political process—education of voters on issues; upgrading the quality of political machines; restoring honor to public office; adequate compensation in order to make graft unnecessary, and proper supervision to minimize graft; the development and use of consultative services to supplement the inadequate experience of local officials; and the experimenting with new political forms to meet the special needs of metropolitan areas.

This is not an easy task. It calls for great dedication, and much expenditure of time and energy. At times it may demand renunciation of special favors that we have been receiving in the easy give-and-take of local politics. But if we can revivify local and state governments, they in turn can work out programs of co-ordination for meeting needs now handled by Federal authorities. They can present to the voters a real alternative—a choice between local and Federal control of services that citizens want.

The lack of such an approach will doom the conservative voice in the United States to angry impotence. The liberal centralizer will cite needs. If the only conservative answer is to say that a rich nation cannot afford to meet these needs, it is probable that the majority of voters will reluctantly favor the candidate who promises action. It may be a reluctant vote, since voters are also taxpayers.

If American conservatism declines into a whining minority being unwillingly dragged into the twentieth century, our nation will suffer a great loss. For there is real merit in the conservative protest against ever-increasing Federal power. But conservatives should realize that mere protest is not enough. They must give leadership in developing a realistic alternative method for meeting the needs of a growing nation in a troubled world.

We Catholics should give considerable thought to this problem. Love of country is a virtue, and one that should be exercised at all times, and not merely in periods of war or great danger. And we exercise this virtue, not by incessant denunciations—these become boring and even irritating—but by consistent and intelligent effort to rebuild and perfect the all important local foundations of our Democracy.

VII

The Catholic Image in Economic Life

Economic Growth

Currently we have many discussions about economic growth. It is a subject well worth careful study. But how should it be studied? merely as an economic issue? as a matter of political policy? or as a moral problem?

Actually, as in so many concrete issues, all three elements are involved. No treatment that neglected any of these points would be complete. There are, however, good reasons in this chapter for stressing the moral and economic, and underplaying the political. We can be sure that the last-named will be more than fully treated in partisan controversy. But the other aspects may be by-passed.

One significant moral factor was raised again and again by Pope Pius XII. In his social writings he frequently objected to a purely materialistic and quantitative view of economic life. He did not like to see people treated as masses, quantities to be manipulated according to formulas and tables.

Nor was the pope happy at efforts to make production an end in itself, without regard to what was produced or how it was made—with the notion, more specifically, that it makes little difference in terms of national income and national product whether we produce more and more

149

luxuries for those already surfeited, or necessities for those in need, since both processes produce income and employment.

Yet there is a significant difference in the result insofar as it affects people. If our economy were merely to grow faster, but along the same lines it followed in recent years, certain results can be predicted. More and more families would become middle-class. They would have two cars, two television sets, and possibly even two homes, if we count a summer cottage at a beach.

But in the process of growth, we would expect a still higher percentage of married women to be working. The already high percentage of working mothers of small children would increase. There would be less parental supervision of the family and more and more teen-agers with cars, money, and little obvious purpose in life.

If our emphasis were mainly upon material gains and increase in luxuries, there would be the danger of a certain erosion of national purpose and will. High living standards of themselves need not produce such a result, but the danger is great that luxury and wealth may be abused. Certainly we cannot assume as an unquestioned axiom that the amassing of wealth should be our main goal in life.

Paradoxically, while the bulk of Americans would be moving into the middle class, we would expect pockets of serious poverty and even exploitation to persist. About one-fourth of our families would be receiving income below any decent minimum level. There would be slums and all the social ills that they breed. It has been clearly evident in recent years that prosperity does not seep down, even slowly, to certain elements in our population.

Furthermore, as our living standards increased, the contrast between our way of life and the destitution endemic throughout much of the world would increase. While living conditions in Asia, Africa, and Latin America would rise by absolute standards, relatively they would lag farther and farther behind our own. This fact not only poses a problem of conscience, it is also a source of possible deep political discontent.

Given these trends, it is understandable that many American writers are questioning the goals we have set for ourselves. They ask why, in an affluent society, we have such serious pockets of poverty. They further question our relative neglect of public sectors of the economy, if we may so class such problems as slums, our educational standards, and the availability of medical care.

The writers we refer to, and their political counterparts, have a solution for the problems they have noted. They would have government step in at two levels, first to force a higher growth rate upon our economy, and secondly to distribute much of this increment into the public sector as defined above.

This prescription raises important questions in both the economic and the political spheres. Perhaps the first question that should be raised is a question of fact. It is assumed that our economy is presently stagnating, with growth just about matching population gains. Those who hold this view marshal impressive statistical evidence to bolster their argument.

Yet these statistics seem to contradict the evidence of our eyes. We can see in almost any area of the land the

151

growth of new suburbs, with consequent heavy public expenditures for schools, roads, and other necessary facilities. More and more of our farms are being gobbled up for housing subdivisions or great shopping centers. Indeed, it is predicted that before long, there will be a solid metropolitan region ranging from Boston to Richmond.

In addition to quantitative expansion, there are remarkable qualitative changes. There are quite a few major corporations in the United States the bulk of whose production centers on products unknown two decades ago. New plastics, synthetic fibers, and electronic equipment are well known illustrations.

Furthermore, overall averages on growth are likely to be quite deceptive. This is especially true when one compares growth rates in the United States with those of the Soviet Union. Is it significant that Soviet coal production surpasses our own? After all, we deliberately chose to substitute oil and gas for coal in home heating.

Likewise, it would be meaningless were Soviet production of grains to better ours. As is well known, we have surpluses far beyond any conceivable needs. We are actually choosing to cut back in many areas of production. There will be declines in coal mining, grain output, and railroad carloadings. While these losses may lower national averages of production, they certainly are no indications of stagnation.

By contrast, if we look at areas in which we want to grow, the rate of increase is often fantastic, ranging from twenty to forty per cent annually, or even higher. There are large corporations today that did not exist ten years ago. The output and effect of electronic computers are little short of revolutionary. Air transport, both freight and passenger, grows at a tremendous rate. Such items as electric typewriters, transistor radios, television sets, and high-fidelity phonographs are all products that have grown up since World War II.

Substantially speaking, these growth areas are private, not public. There was some public participation insofar as military interest and contracts at times occasioned the basic research needed. But most often the military merely noted the need, and left private ingenuity to come up with the product wanted.

American experience was duplicated in Europe and Asia. Nations (such as Germany and Japan) that emphasized private initiative, showed remarkable rates of growth. If one were to compare West German and Soviet postwar growth, thus concentrating on nations that were substantially devastated during the War, West Germany would clearly be the winner in the contest.

On the basis of these observations, it is by no means evident that the solution to our own problems is either forced growth by government intervention, or forced diversion of our resources into the public sector of the economy. In the light of Soviet experience, we can hardly state that a regimented economy is completely inefficient. But the drive and initiative of a free society seem to get better and quicker results.

There are two vital elements of economic productivity that flourish better in the private sector. These are initiative and competitive drive. Government enterprise by its very nature does not encourage initiative. There are so many necessary controls, and checks and balances, that

153

routine and unimaginative effort tends to be the norm. Even in the Soviet system, plant managers have been forced into a private-enterprise type of side deals in the attempt to meet their quotas.

Government enterprise also lacks the element of competition. It is interesting to contrast the action of a large corporation, which recently released a top executive and forced him to restore profits made by side dealings, with the inaction in the face of revelations of military waste. We do not assert that private enterprise is free of inefficiency, waste, featherbedding, collusive deals, and the like. But we do note that the competitive system tends to correct these abuses.

The basic fallacy in the arguments favoring economic growth by forced government action is the assumption that federal tinkering will necessarily make the patient better. Unquestionably there are real problems in our economy. Where poverty exists in a rich nation, through no fault of the individuals concerned, something has gone wrong.

But it would seem to be a matter of common sense that our first approach to such problems would be direct, a study of causes and remedies based on careful analysis of all the factors involved. It does not seem reasonable to make drastic changes in an economic system that is conceded to be the best in the world, because in certain aspects it is imperfect.

The massive shifts into public enterprise demanded by certain writers would involve a real change in our economic system. The present burden of taxes is near the critical point. We certainly have the right to demand more proof than is currently offered before we adopt policies of forced growth. We need proof that methods advocated will stimulate healthy growth, and not just inflation. And we need proof that they would do it better than the present method.

These points will be pursued further in the following chapter, with emphasis upon the causes of poverty in our rich nation.

Poverty in Our Midst

In discussing economic growth, we noted that in this rich nation many millions of families live in poverty. About one-third of our families, including unattached individuals, have incomes of less than $4,000 a year. Over seven million in this class received less than $2,000 cash income in 1958. On the basis of these raw figures, one might conclude that the problem is indeed appalling.

Yet the average American is likely to be sceptical about any such conclusion. If such destitution exists, where are these utterly wretched people hiding themselves? Some years ago, a visiting Italian prelate asked this writer to show him the slums of Washington. On driving through these areas, he asked who owned the automobiles parked in front of the homes. He was told that the poor people owned them, or at least were making finance payments upon them. He was quite confused by the whole situation.

In all likelihood, he underestimated the problem by this superficial tour. Had he entered the homes, seen the terrible overcrowding, and noted that diet and medical care were quite inadequate, he would not have been so quick to conclude that we ride to the poor houses in Cadillacs. There is real poverty in the United States, although not to the degree that the statistics quoted above would suggest.

The difficulty in using cash income as an indication of how poor we are lies in the numerous special situations that are concealed in overall figures. An aged person, living alone, may have accumulated a substantial amount of savings. He may own his own home. His needs for clothing and entertainment may be modest. As a result, he may live adequately on an annual $2,000 return from investments, with very little dipping into his savings. Statistically he appears quite poor; actually he has few financial worries.

At the other end of the age spectrum, we may find a young married couple who have no current earnings of any importance. The husband is going through medical school. The wife is taking care of their young children. They will be able through loans and help from their families to make things meet until the husband is able to practice medicine. Since loans are not normally classed as income, they likewise are statistically poor. In fact, their lifetime income prospects are quite good.

Again, we may find a farmer whose cash income is quite low. But he owns the farm and its property. He can take care of most of his own food needs from the products he raises. His wife may contribute by sewing clothes for herself and the girls. Here likewise, the bare listing of cash income would be misleading in terms of actual living standards.

In the situations just described, we note that there can

be serious error in judging from general averages. There are other cases in which the poverty is real enough, but where the causes may be factors other than economic. In such cases, no amount of general economic growth, whether natural or forced by government action, will make much difference. They are out of the mainstream of productive economic life.

Such certainly would be the case with many seriously handicapped persons. The blind, the totally deaf, the crippled, those suffering from serious mental illness, those lacking in normal intelligence, and many similar persons may find their earning ability quite limited. It is a good thing to "hire the handicapped" and efforts to train them to be productive are most salutary. But there still remain millions of persons whose best efforts will earn them only limited incomes.

There are also persons suffering from personality defects that are not normally classed as mental illnesses. Alcoholics often find it hard to hold a good job. There are the drifters and floaters that beg and do odd jobs in our large cities. Some workers are careless and irresponsible, and hence usually drift lower and lower in the economic scale. Our nation could become fabulously rich, and yet these unfortunates would still live in poverty.

Other workers suffer from illiteracy or language difficulties. A person who cannot read or write is not likely to get a well-paying job. This may be at least a temporary obstacle for those who do not know English. Until they get a good command of our language, they are not likely to be paid as much as their energy and intelligence might warrant.

157

Racial discrimination is still another factor in income levels. In many areas of the country, there is a twofold discrimination against minorities, and especially Negroes. They are barred from certain good jobs. And often they get paid less for their work than would a white worker doing the same task. Moreover, discrimination often leads to poorer education, and hence decreased ability to do skilled or even semi-skilled work. We deplore this bias, but the remedy is not usually economic.

Even where the causes of poverty are clearly economic, it does not always follow that general economic growth will help in certain particular situations. For example, the West Virginia situation was highly publicized during the presidential primary of 1960. But there are many like areas throughout the nation. Either a decline in demand for the product, or movements of an entire industry, have left cities and regions in abject poverty.

No matter how we may speed up general economic growth, the effect upon such areas is likely to be slight and much delayed. If their basic industry is permanently depressed, there are only two feasible solutions to the problem of poverty and unemployment. Either new industries must come in, or workers must move to areas where jobs are more likely to be available. General growth might help in this process, especially if a real labor shortage developed. But the impact would be rather slow, the more so when one considers the human misery involved.

When a displaced worker is over forty years of age, he runs into special difficulties in getting suitable employment. Many employers do not want to hire older workers. Some say that it is not easy to retrain them. Or they may create problems in terms of a pension system. The Department of Labor and the Fraternal Order of Eagles have made commendable efforts to persuade employers to hire older workers. Direct efforts of this type, rather than general force-feeding of the economy, seem to be the answer to this problem.

The same observations apply to the two or three million marginal farm families. They lack land, capital for machinery, or experienced managerial ability. Consequently they are likely to remain low-income problems, no matter what solution is ultimately found for the farm problem. Indeed, one of the reasons why Congress has not come up with a better answer to farm economics is unwillingness to face this fact. It would be socially desirable that such families remain on the land, but they must be given opportunities to earn their income from sources other than farming.

Finally, we may list low-income families and individuals whose plight is exclusively caused by inadequate economic growth. We envision a young husband, with no physical or emotional handicaps, working in a steel mill. He is laid off because of inadequate demand, compounded by the higher efficiency of newly automated mills. He does not know when he will be recalled. He has bought his home and does not want to move elsewhere to seek work. He definitely would be benefitted by a general pickup in the economy.

The analysis just given is not an argument against sound economic growth or rising living standards. The point rather is one of advising caution in our expectations. Regardless of promises made in party platforms or during a political campaign, it would not be easy for any administration to abolish poverty in the United States. Even if our economy were to approach the levels set by West Germany, where there is an actual deficit of workers, we would still have millions who would be unable to rise from the bottom of the economic ladder.

Another lesson from this analysis is the need to look behind statistics and generalizations. Total numbers of unemployed, of persons on relief, or of families beneath a given income level can give a misleading impression of the actual state of our economy. If these figures are used cynically for partisan debate, there is little likelihood that lasting damage will be done. But if they are used as guides for public policy, then real harm could ensue.

Unfortunately, a large number of American economists seem to paint with broad brushes. They like overall figures and overall remedies. They are like physicians with their favorite broadband antibiotics, to be used with abandon. Most of us prefer that our internists find our precise ailments and prescribe accordingly. Let us hope that equal precision is used to meet our problem of poverty and economic growth.

Our Christian conscience bids us to do all within our power to help the poor and unfortunate in our midst. But the best form of aid is that which is tailored to the needs of these persons. Shotgun remedies may bring little help, and can also involve real dangers for the economic system. There is no substitute for careful thought and intelligent planning.

Medical Bills for the Aged

In the preceding section we mentioned medical care for the aged as an example of a difficult problem currently facing our nation. We noted that it is not easy to generalize a solution that is adequate for an issue of such complexity. We now go into this subject more deeply, as a case history in Catholic social thinking.

As always, we are concerned with both facts and principles. Among the pertinent facts are these: medical care is far more expensive today than it was fifty years ago, even allowing for a shrinkage in the value of the dollar; people live longer today, thanks largely to the better quality of medical care; for various reasons, many children are unable or unwilling to take care of aged parents as guests in their homes.

Some of these older persons are able to work and to support themselves. But very many are either unable to work or unable to find jobs. In spite of every effort to persuade employers to hire older workers, the emphasis today is upon youth. As automation increases, there is less likelihood that senior workers will have the needed skills.

Income and savings vary among the elderly who cannot work for one reason or another. Almost sixty per cent of aged individuals, in 1958, had cash incomes of $1,000 or less. Between fifteen and twenty per cent had cash incomes over $2,000, which can be considered as a meager minimum for existence. Even with every allowance for social security and private pensions, only a small percentage of the aged can live properly on *current* income.

There remains the possibility that these persons have savings in adequate amounts. Yet in 1958, sixty percent of persons over sixty-five had less than $5,000 in liquid assets. Those who own their homes, of course, have an important asset. The same applies to insurance policies, but these, by their very nature, should not be drawn upon for current needs.

The factual picture seems to indicate that a great majority of older persons will have difficulty in meeting basic needs for food, clothing, and housing out of current incomes. When chronic illness strikes such a person or family, with bills easily mounting into the thousands, the result is financial disaster. They need outside help.

In many cases, fortunately, this help is available from their children. But some couples have no children. In other cases, the children do not have the resources to meet heavy medical costs. They may have a hard time paying bills for their own families. They may be sons or daughters in religious communities. Unfortunately, there are even some cases of children who could help but lack the filial piety to be willing to assist their parents.

Where the family cannot or will not help, the aged person must seek aid from charity, either private or public. In theory, at least, no aged person need starve, become homeless, or lack adequate medical care. In practice, even casual glances at stories in the daily press indicate that many do fall into neglect and destitution.

These are the facts, so far as they are known today. Those who wish to probe more deeply into this aspect of the problem can ask their Senator for Senate Report No. 1121, of the 1960 session.

Other pertinent data should include the fact that none of the bills proposed to help the aged would meet all their medical needs. At the most, they would provide medical, surgical, hospital, and nursing-home care in limited amounts. A chronic invalid who needs continual nursing-home care, or a companion at all times at home, would not be aided by proposed legislation.

How would a voter, or a legislator, approach this problem in the light of the moral and social teachings of our Church? First and most important, he would recognize that it is *his* problem, at least in part. He may not, as a Christian, be indifferent to the needs of his neighbor. It is permissible to say that the first responsibility lies with the aged themselves and with their children. But if this response does not really answer the need, then a problem of Christian charity arises.

Even when the aged may be physically able and willing to help themselves, they may be unable to find work. If we are employers, here is a problem that may well trouble our consciences. Our firm may contribute generously to the United Givers' Fund or similar agencies. But it might be better to help the aged in a form that will let them keep their self-respect. A small loss on a less productive older worker could be a real form of charity.

Through community agencies we could study possibilities for more employment of the aged. Campaigns to hire the handicapped have proved successful. One large service organization is concentrating upon jobs for workers over forty. It may well be proved that traditional barriers to older workers could be surmounted, with proper interest, effort, ingenuity.

This brings up an aspect of Christian charity that is often overlooked. Charity is helping the *person,* not necessarily the need. One could throw food at a starving beggar. This would meet his physical needs, but it would insult his human dignity. Would Christ act in this way?

We know the phrase "It is more blessed to give than to receive." But we often fail to realize that it is often easier to give than to receive. One of the most basic urges in human nature is the desire for independence. This is almost the essence of maturity and adulthood, and its beginnings show in early childhood. We hurt people deeply, at times at least, when we force them into a status of dependence upon the mercy of others.

This hurt can be lessened somewhat when kindness is personal. We all recognize the fact that, in our modern complex society, there is a need for relatively impersonal social agencies. But we as Catholics should always strive to decrease this need, and to keep alive the principle of direct Christian love of neighbor in all forms of assistance.

Returning to the immediate problem of medical care for the aged, we could hardly discharge our responsibilities merely by stating the principle that aid for the needy should be direct and personal. The point is that such aid may not be available in adequate amounts at the present time. We may not call upon Christian principles of charity as a subterfuge for evading our obligations in this same charity.

Since it is unlikely that God-fearing and benevolent persons will take care of the needs of all the aged in a direct manner, what is the next step in our thinking? Generally it is that the government should step in and meet the problem. If it is wrong to be always running to the public treasury as a solution for problems, it is equally reprobate to refuse such assistance in the case of genuine need, not met by private resources.

The question then arises, upon what principle should we base public assistance to the needy aged? Should government step in only when there is demonstrated need? Or should it take steps to forestall this need? Here is the major distinction between the two approaches that have been before Congress. A second distinction involves the respective roles of the Federal and state governments.

Here a person influenced by the social philosophy of the Church runs into conflicting principles. The bills that advocate tying medical aid into the Social Security system involve the principle of prepayment and insurance. Social Security funds in this context would not be charity to the indigent aged. They would be payment of a form of medical insurance to which these persons contributed in their years of productive work. Catholic social thinkers generally favor the principle that the wage-earner should earn enough to take care of medical needs, rather than depend upon charity.

On the other hand, many fear that introducing medical care into the Old Age and Survivors branch of Social Security will be the beginning of a general program of Federal medical insurance. They object to federalizing a program that should be handled by individual initiative in the first instance, and by private charity and local government where individual resources fail.

Once again, we see the complexity of concrete social issues and the difficulty of meeting them by broad social principles, such as those of the living wage, on the one hand, and those of states' rights and individual initiative, on the other. Both principles have their validity. The difficulty in the concrete is to discover which should prevail in order to insure the common good of the community.

The Catholic organizations most directly concerned with the problem—the National Conference of Catholic Charities and the Catholic Hospital Association—have reacted differently when faced with the problem of medical care for the aged. The National Conference of Catholic Charities favors a federal program within the framework of social security. The Catholic Hospital Association has not yet taken a public stand on the controversy.

Most Catholic experts who have spoken out on this issue favor the prepayment and insurance rather than the welfare approach. They have seen the agonies of those who had to sell all they owned to obtain meager public or private assistance. While supporting the vital work of voluntary organizations and the special contribution of Christian charity, they feel that prepayment and insurance contribute to the dignity and independence of the needy aged.

Since the experts are not unanimous, we shall not try to prejudge the issue. But we offer a few suggestions that seem to us to be motivated by a Christian attitude toward the problem. First, we would try to do all we could by private initiative. This would involve better hiring policies for aged workers, better private medical insurance, and better private pension plans. We would vitalize and make attractive direct personal help for the needy aged. Catholic lay organizations are especially suited to making this a major study and action project. When government help is considered necessary, we would give the nod to prepayment and insurance plans as more consistent with the dignity of our aged citizens. We do this knowing that it does involve an enhancement of Federal action in the broad field of welfare. But we would seek for formulae that try to safeguard to the utmost the work of states, cities, and voluntary agencies.

No prospective solution is perfect. But this demonstration of the complexity of the problem might teach us a certain reserve and even humility in urging our own point of view. In issues of this type, it may be difficult to say who is right. But we instinctively feel that the arrogant dogmatist is wrong. Life is just not that simple.

The Church and Labor

Labor Day each year should be more than a secular holiday. It should also be an occasion for recalling the deep interest the Church has shown toward workers. In the United States we have special permission to offer on that day the Mass of St. Joseph, the Worker. Many dioceses use this feast for special Labor Day Masses and sermons.

To understand the concern for the Church, and especially of recent popes, for workers, it is necessary to recall some nineteenth-century history. This was the century that felt the full impact of the Industrial Revolution. It was a time of great vitality, with railroads drastically changing modes of travel and new factories bringing entirely different methods and techniques of production.

Like all revolutions, it was deeply unsettling to the participants. Cities grew up almost overnight around factory complexes. Commerce thrived, but often ground to a halt because of financial speculation. Millions of workers left the relative security of the farm for the riskier toil at machines.

In the frantic race for profits, labor was often exploited. It was not uncommon for children of six or seven years to work in factories. Women did heavy labor in the mines. For adult male workers, hours of work were long and pay was often poor. Some of our readers may remember that the twelve-hour day, seven-day week, in the heat of the steel mills, was changed only in the present century.

The harsh conditions surrounding the new factories drew varied reactions. Those who grew rich from the mills tended to consider poverty and slums as necessary evils. Some ministers of religion found the Will of God in the situation. Solemn professors argued that unchanging laws of economics made these evils beyond the power of man to remedy. Any intervention would make matters worse.

The Socialists were quite willing to accept this analysis, twisting it to support their view that capitalism was beyond reform. To them the only solution was the abolition of private property, the so-called root of exploitation. Marx said that this could be accomplished only through revolution. For this purpose he preached the gospel of class hatred.

Others favored a more moderate approach. They attempted through social legislation and labor organization to better the condition of workers. They tried to regulate child labor. They sought protection for working women. And they formed unions to fight for labor's rights.

Thus, at the end of the century, there was a three-way pull upon economic society. Capitalists favored the existing state of things. Some workers chose socialism. Others, often inspired by Christian ideals of love of neighbor, sought reform rather than revolution.

In the midst of this confusion, Rome spoke. On May 15, 1891, Leo XIII issued his great encyclical letter "On the Condition of Workers." This document burst upon the world with the explosive force of a hydrogen bomb. To each camp the Pope issued words of warning and counsel.

To the factory owners he said: "Workers are not to be treated as slaves; justice demands that the dignity of the human personality be respected in them, ennobled as it has been through what we call the Christian character." He condemned the inequitable distribution of wealth: "The present age handed over the workers, each alone and defenseless, to the inhumanity of employers and the unbridled greed of competitors. . . . A very few rich and exceedingly rich men have laid a yoke almost of slavery on the unnumbered masses of nonowning workers."

He strongly condemned Socialism and class hatred and defended the right of private property. Socialism would injure the workers, depriving them of all hope of ownership and making them dependent upon the state. Class struggle is unnatural: "Each needs the other completely; neither capital can do without labor, nor labor without capital. Concord begets beauty and order in things."

To workers the Pope noted both their right to organize into unions and their right to a wage suitable for their needs. He denounced abuses in the hiring of women and children: "It is not right to demand of a woman or a child what a strong adult man is capable of doing or would be willing to do. . . . For budding strength in childhood, like greening verdure in spring, is crushed by premature harsh treatment; and under such circumstances all education of the child must needs be foregone. Certain occupations likewise are less fitted for women, who are intended by nature for the work of the home."

Today some of these observations may seem commonplace. Others may appear unduly harsh upon employers and the rich. But in 1891, they offered guidance sorely needed by the world of that time. Society was moving toward a point of decision. There had to be either reform or revolution. The exploitation and insecurity of the period had reached a point that made change unavoidable.

The genius of Pope Leo XIII lay in the fact that he clearly stated the need for change, yet insisted upon the moderate course of reform rather than revolution. His thinking had a profound impact upon much of Europe. Indeed, Pope Pius XI noted that the labor philosophy incorporated into the Treaty of Versailles was taken almost verbatim from the letter of his predecessor.

The early years of the twentieth century did bring reforms. There was social legislation, especially in England, France, and Germany. Unions were formed and some became strong. Certain employers, inspired by Christian ideals, voluntarily sought to better the condition of their workers. In the Church there were strong attempts to form a body of social teaching inspired by Christian ideals.

Yet other forces were also at work. While conditions at the factory improved, speculation in the stock markets of the world rampaged unchecked. High finance was guilty of gross abuses. These culminated in the worldwide economic depression that reached its low point in 1931. At this point, another pope, Pius XI, issued another encyclical, on the fortieth anniversary of Pope Leo's letter, this one entitled "On Reconstructing the Social Order."

Pope Pius XI reaffirmed the teaching of his predecessor. He was even more powerful in denouncing the financial abuses that caused millions to be hungry and unemployed. He demanded drastic changes in the direction of social responsibility on the part of capital. Otherwise, he said, nothing could stem the forces of revolution being fed from the Communist world. His defense of unionism was strong. And he made precise the demand for a living wage for workers, indicating that it must be sufficient to support a worker and his family in decent comfort.

He went beyond his predecessor in calling for capital-labor collaboration. He asked that this be placed on an organized basis and made part of the very structure of society. He preferred that needed reforms be achieved by joint action of workers and owners, and not thrust upon an already overburdened government.

The impact of this historic document was tremendous. The worldwide depression had shaken the confidence of many in the capitalist system. The appeal of Socialism and Communism was growing. Rome once again charted the road to moderation. No voice was stronger than the pope's in denouncing the abuses of the times. Yet he was insistent that the economic system be reformed, not de-

171

molished by any kind of violent revolutionary action.

In fact, change did sweep the world in varying degrees. The United States had its New Deal. Social legislation advanced in France and England. Germany, Italy, Spain, and Portugal had authoritarian governments. And then came World War II.

The advent of the war coincided with the election of a new pope. Pius XII began his reign in sorrow, as his children destroyed one another. When the war was over, the demand for additional social reform was great. Organized labor had reached a new pinnacle of power, and was exercising political influence in many nations of the world.

Since many European unions were Socialist-inspired, this power was often exercised in the direction of Socialist ideas. Because of this, Pope Pius XII, while reaffirming his predecessors' stand on labor organization and social reform, felt the need for words of caution. Immediately after the war, he warned against the trend toward nationalizing industry. He felt that this would enhance dangerous concentrations of power.

In 1950, he warned against pushing programs for social reform too far. Labor should not repeat the mistake of capital in the preceding century, concentrating more and more power in the hands of either government or central labor bodies. He warned German Catholics against seeking the right of joint-management of industry for labor organizations. To Belgian workers he warned that "The temptation to abuse the force of organization is a temptation as strong and as dangerous as that of abusing the power of private capital."

In 1954, he told the International Labor Organization

that labor "cannot visualize its future in terms of opposition to other social classes or of the excessive ascendancy of the state over the individual."

Once again, Rome endorses the way of moderation and principle. It fights for the legitimate rights of all, and against abuses from any source. The popes champion the principle of labor organization. But when labor abuses its power, it is rebuked and warned, as capital was warned of its neglect and selfishness.

In a word, the Church is above all classes. It is for justice and charity. It will side with the oppressed, but will not support them if they in turn become oppressors. This balance and wisdom is badly needed by the world. Society can always learn from the inspired wisdom of Peter's successors.

Suggested Reading

The titles listed below were selected primarily to stimulate our thinking as Catholics in the areas treated in this book.

Religious and Spiritual

CASTELOT, JOHN J., S.S. *Meet the Bible.* Baltimore: Helicon, 1960-1963. Three volumes of popular introduction to the Holy Scriptures. The first two volumes treat of the Old Testament and the last considers the New Testament.

HUESMAN, ROSE M. *Saints in Aprons.* Milwaukee: Bruce, 1962. A housewife investigates the problem of sanctity, as seen from the viewpoint of her family duties.

KNOX, RONALD A. *The Layman and His Conscience.* New York: Sheed and Ward, 1961. Monsignor Knox considers the relation between the Christian and the great spiritual realities. He suggests how these may be integrated into a pattern of life.

The Lay Apostolate

GEANEY, DENNIS J., O.S.A. *Christians in a Changing World.* Chicago: Fides, 1959. The apostolate of the layman in a world of changing social, cultural, and religious values. A stimulus to fresh thinking.

CONGAR, YVES, O.P. *Laity, Church, and World.* Baltimore: Helicon, 1960. A brief study of the role of the laity in the Church. Notes the freedom, responsibility, and growing mission of the layman today.

LECLERCQ, JACQUES. *Christians in the World.* New York: Sheed and Ward, 1961. How the layman faces the modern world through personal sanctity and an effort to put Christian ideals into society. Stresses the social aspects of religion.

174

DOHEN, DOROTHY. *Women in Wonderland.* New York: Sheed and Ward, 1960. The American woman and her problems. The theology of woman applied to various states of life chosen or providentially imposed on women.

THORMAN, DONALD J. *The Emerging Layman.* New York: Doubleday, 1962. Aspects of the lay apostolate in contemporary America. A good book for stimulating insight into possibilities for effective Catholic action.

The Ecumenical Movement

SCHARPER, PHILIP. *American Catholics: A Protestant-Jewish View.* New York: Sheed and Ward, 1959. A frank symposium by two Jewish and four Protestant authors, with concluding reflections by Father Gustave Weigel, S.J. Centers on the problem of authority.

TAVARD, GEORGE H. *Two Centuries of Ecumenicism.* Notre Dame: Fides, 1960; Mentor Omega, 1962. A good historical background for current ecumenical moves following from Vatican Council II. Father Tavard treats of principal interreligious contacts, mainly in Europe and the United States.

BAUM, GREGORY, O.S.A. *Progress and Perspectives.* New York: Sheed and Ward, 1962. A strong call for Christian renewal, especially within the Catholic Church, as a stimulus for understanding and unity.

KÜNG, HANS. *The Council, Reform, and Reunion.* New York: Sheed and Ward, 1961. The controversial proposals of a young but brilliant theologian as he faces the needs of the Church in a world seeking Christian reunion.

Race Relations

AHMANN, MATHEW (ed.). *Race; Challenge to Religion.* Chicago: Regnery, 1963. The major papers read at the historic National Conference on Race and Religion. A joint religious testament to a common ideal of justice and love in race relations.

SENSER, ROBERT. *Primer on Interracial Justice.* Baltimore: Helicon, 1962. Some practical observations on both the theories and the problems affecting race relations. Very helpful for beginners in this field.

McMANUS, EUGENE P., S.S.J. *Studies in Race Relations.* Baltimore: Josephite Press, 1961. Theory and practice for the Catholic interested in racial problems. Contains study club material and many valuable quotations.

O'NEILL, JOSEPH E., S.J. (ed.). *A Catholic Case Against Segregation*. New York: Macmillan, 1961. Six Jesuit scholars examine various social, legal, and political aspects of segregation, as well as its moral status. A solid treatment for those who seek a deeper insight into this problem.

Social Problems

THOMAS, JOHN L., S.J. *The Catholic Viewpoint on Marriage and the Family*. Garden City, N.Y.: Hanover, 1958. Father Thomas is one of the leading Catholic sociologists and edits a well known weekly column on family problems. A competent study of marriage and family problems.

McCLUSKEY, NEIL G., S.J. *Catholic Viewpoint on Education*. Garden City, N.Y.: Hanover House, 1959. Various aspects of Catholic education at the primary and secondary levels, including federal aid and other problems affecting our schools.

KERWIN, JEROME. *Catholic Viewpoint on Church and State*. Garden City, N.Y.: Hanover House, 1960. A Chicago University professor offers a penetrating treatment of Catholic principles on Church-State relations. In addition he gives pertinent American aspects of the problem.

MURRAY, JOHN COURTNEY, S.J. *We Hold These Truths*. New York: Sheed and Ward, 1960. Father Murray is one of our most original and stimulating Catholic thinkers in the area of politics. He applies his principles to the American consensus. A stimulating book on American democracy.

CRONIN, JOHN F., S.S. *Social Principles and Economic Life*. Milwaukee: Bruce, 1959. The social teaching of the Catholic Church, applied to American social and economic problems.

GREELEY, ANDREW M. *The Church and the Suburbs*. New York: Sheed and Ward, 1959. Father Greeley faces the special problems of suburban living, as they affect Christian living. He feels that we need new approaches to meet this situation.

MURRAY, THOMAS E. *Nuclear Policy for War and Peace*. Cleveland: World Publishing Co., 1960. One of the leading Catholic experts on atomic problems argues that we are being controlled by technology rather than by moral considerations in fashioning atomic policy.

HARRINGTON, MICHAEL. *The Other America: Poverty in the U.S.* New York: Macmillan, 1962. A graphically written study of poverty in the U.S., and perhaps one of the most extensive studies on the subject.